THE WORLD WE WISH TO SEE

THE WORLD WE WISH TO SEE

Revolutionary Objectives in the Twenty-First Century

Samir Amin

translated by
James Membrez

AAKAR

THE WORLD WE WISH TO SEE
Samir Amin

Published in agreement with Monthly Review Press, New York
for publication and sale only in the Indian Subcontinent
(India, Pakistan, Bangladesh, Nepal, Maldives,
Bhutan & Sri Lanka)

First Published in India, 2009

Published by
AAKAR BOOKS
28 E Pocket IV, Mayur Vihar Phase I, Delhi-110 091
Phone : 011-2279 5505 Telefax : 011-2279 5641
aakarbooks@gmail.com; www.aakarbooks.com

Printed at
S.N. Pritners, G-28, Sector 2, Bawana, Delhi 110 039

CONTENTS

PREFACE

Capitalism is a world system. Its victims can effectively face its challenges only if they are also organized at the global level. However, the unequal development associated with the global spread of capital has always presented serious difficulties for the internationalism of peoples. Here, I propose to identify the origin and nature of the obstacles that impede a convergence of today's diverse struggles against capitalist domination and exploitation.

THE OBJECTIVE FOUNDATIONS OF DIVERSITY IN GLOBAL CAPITALISM

Capitalism is the fundamental mode of production that defines the modern period. It is based on the class conflict between labor and capital. This conflict is the basis for the proletarian character proclaimed by the international organizations of the popular classes engaged in anti-capitalist social struggles. It is also the basis for the socialist (or communist) horizon by which the proletariat in question has defined its liberation. It is thus quite natural that proletarian internationalism originated in the advanced centers of the world capitalist system in nineteenth-century Western Europe. However, the affirmation of this dominant reality has contributed to hiding the imperialist character of global capitalist expansion and the unique characteristics of social struggles in the peripheries of the system.

The diversity of social and political conditions in the states and nations that make up the world system results from the nature of the development of global capitalism. More particularly, this involves: 1. the inherent contrast between the centers and the peripheries in this development—in other words, the fundamentally imperialist nature of this expansion in every phase of its history; and 2. the multiplicity of centers constituted as historical nation-states, which are engaged in continual competition with each other. Despite being subordinated to the requirements of accumulation in the centers of the system, the social formations of the peripheries have never been marked by the central position of the industrial proletariat in the whole organization of production. Peasant societies that are subjected to the logic of imperialist expansion are just as much victims of the system as are, to various degrees, other classes and social groups.

Throughout the course of their formation, nations, whether dominant or dominated, have always been marked by their own distinctive characteristics and specific peculiarities. Hence, the hegemonic blocs of classes and interests that have made it possible for capital to establish its domination, as well as the blocs which the victims of the system have constructed, have always differed from one country to another and one era to another. This has produced particular political cultures, articulating, in their own way, systems of values and traditions comprised of specific forms of expression, organization, and struggle. These diverse values and traditions are also objective, just like the cultures through which they are expressed. Finally, the development of the productive forces through scientific and technological revolutions has governed, in turn, changes in the organization of labor and the diverse forms of labor's subjection to the demands of capitalist exploitation.

The totality of these diverse realities precludes reducing the political actors on the world stage to simply the bourgeoisie and proletariat. Such a simplification, which perhaps livens up polemics, never permits the implementation of an effective politics. This diversity, since it is objective, produces a segmentation of the popular classes and other dominated and exploited peoples, which generates fragmentation within their resistance struggles—

even offensive struggles that succeed in modifying the balance of power to their advantage.

Diversity does not favor a natural convergence of struggles against what will be seen, only after the fact, to have been the principal adversary. On the contrary, it accentuates the potentially negative consequences of immediate conflicts of interest, such as conflicts between urban and rural workers (around, for example, the price of food) and conflicts between nations or dominant national blocs.

The strategies of the dominant powers for reproducing their position have often successfully exploited the negative effects of this segmentation of interests and struggles. The flexibility of capitalism, often analyzed as the expression of its exceptional power (compared with the rigidity—real or mythical—of other systems), is hardly more than the expression of the requirements for its reproduction as the dominant pole within conditions of continual diversity and evolution.

Nationalism frequently reinforces the success of these strategies of capital and the hegemonic bloc that it leads. In the centers of the imperialist system, this happens by way of the rallying of political movements supported by the popular classes to strategies implemented on the world level by the dominant classes. Colonization and imperialist domination have been legitimized in this way—yesterday by the discourse of the "civilizing mission," today by those who pretend to export democracy and defend human rights across the globe. Socialist parties and social democrats have often aligned themselves with these positions and thus deserve to be called social-colonialists (or social-imperialists). This is certainly true of the social-liberal Atlanticists of contemporary Europe. Nationalism has sometimes also been heightened—with success, unfortunately—by the intensification of inter-imperialist conflicts. The popular classes, or at least the parties representing them, have joined forces with their respective bourgeoisies in major conflicts, as happened during the First World War.

In contrast, the situation of the dominated peripheries often gives rise to national liberation movements. These are perfectly legitimate and positive within the long-term perspective of eliminating exploitation and oppression. But these movements also present some dangers and illusions that one cannot choose to overlook. In particular, there is the danger of strengthening forces that represent the exploiting classes within the liberation front, whether those forces already have their assigned place in this front or represent a potential danger for the future.

This remains a major and continual problem in so far as global capitalism, an inherently imperialist system, produces and reproduces the contrast between the imperialist centers and the dominated peripheries and, consequently, forces the latter to confront the challenge through national liberation struggles. We will return later to the challenges confronting peoples today by the current neoliberal project.

CHAPTER ONE

THE INTERNATIONALISM OF PEOPLES IN THE TWENTIETH CENTURY

Diversity in the conditions of reproduction of the different partners of global capitalism has always constituted a major challenge to the success of the struggles undertaken by the victims of the system. The Internationals of the workers' and socialist movements were designed precisely to overcome this major obstacle.

The history of the Internationals begins, nearly a century and a half ago, with the formation of the First International in 1864. It would be useful to draw some lessons from this experience that will enable us to better understand the present challenges and options for strategic action.

The First International, called the International Workingmen's Association, was designed precisely to overcome the emergent separation into national groupings. The European revolutions of 1848 had shown the negative effects of such a separation. The new social subject—the primary victim of the expansion of capitalism in Western and Central Europe, the one whose socialist or communist dream was expressed in 1848—was called the "proletariat." It was made up of a minority gathered in the large factories and mines of the era and a large circle of artisanal workers. Since the new proletariat was still exclusively located in the northwestern part of Europe, and spreading to the United States, this implied that the First International's area of action was, in fact, limited to these regions.

Within these limits, the First International managed the diverse conditions of social and political struggles in a democratic spirit that was advanced for its time. The International Workingmen's Association gathered together organizations of different kinds, embryonic political parties, trade unions, cooperatives, civil society groups, and "personalities" like Marx, Proudhon, and Bakunin. Their areas of activity, analyses of challenges, strategic proposals, visions of the future, and mobilizing ideologies were extremely diverse. The limitations in the concepts of the era can easily be pointed out: the dominant patriarchal view of relations between men and women, ignorance of the rest of the world, and so fourth. One could very well discuss the various ideologies that confronted one another (a nascent Marxism, anarchism, worker spontaneism, etc.), their relevance and potential real effectiveness, and so fourth. But that is certainly not the subject of this work. There is one lesson, above all else, that should be retained from this initial experience: democratic respect for the principle of diversity. This is an important lesson for us today.

The Second International was based on completely different principles. The accelerated proletarianization of the era had given birth to new types of workers' parties, with a relatively significant number of followers and influence on the working class. These parties—including English Labour, the Marxist German Social Democracy, and French revolutionary syndicalism—were different from one another, but were nevertheless united, at least originally, around the objective of replacing the capitalist order with socialism. In hindsight, what emerged was the principle of only "one" party for each country, which would be the carrier of the "correct line," regardless of whether this was, as history was going to demonstrate, moderate reformism or the revolutionary option. Engels and the first Marxist leaders (Karl Kautsky, Antonio Labriola, Georgi Plekhanov) certainly considered these options as proof of progress in relation to the First International, which in part they probably were. The new generation of leaders of the Second International did not always ignore the dangers entailed by the dominant options of the era, as some have hastily maintained.

Still, it remains the case that the limits to democratic practices in the political and social movements led by the parties of the Second International stemmed from these fundamental options.

It is also true that the parties of the Second International, on the whole, drifted in the direction of support for imperialism and nationalism. The Second International took little interest in the colonial question and imperialist expansion. It often legitimized the latter by claiming that it had an objectively positive effect (bringing backward peoples into capitalist modernity). This historical perspective, however, is refuted by the imperialist nature inherent in the global expansion of capitalism. The label "social-imperialist" is perfectly appropriate to describe the consequences of this alignment with linear bourgeois economism. This has remained a characteristic feature of the social democratic parties up to the period following the Second World War with their support for Atlanticism and, afterward, social liberalism.

The drift toward imperialism strengthened the chances of nationalist support for the views of the capitalist ruling class, at least in international relations. As is well known, the parties of the Second International foundered on the chauvinism produced by the First World War.

The Third International was created to correct this drift. It did so, at least partially. In fact, it asserted itself on the world level by supporting the creation of communist parties in all of the peripheries of the world system, declaring the strategic character of the alliance of the "Workers of the West" with the "Peasants of the East." Maoism expressed this development by expanding the call for internationalism to include oppressed peoples alongside proletarians of all countries. Later, the alliance between the Third International, the Non-Aligned Movement born in Bandung,[1] and the Tricontinental[2] reinforced the idea and practice of globalizing anti-capitalist struggles on a truly planetary scale.

Still, the Third International retained and developed the organizational choices of the Second International: a single party for each country, the party as the bearer of the "correct" line, and the party as the catalyst for all demands put forward by trade unions and mass organizations, which were considered to be "transmission belts." The Third International also found itself in a situation unknown to both the First and Second Internationals: it had to defend the first socialist state and later the camp of socialist states.

The Fourth International, formed precisely in reaction to this evolution, was not at all innovative with regard to the organizational forms initiated by the Third International. It supposedly only wanted to return to the original forms.

BANDUNG AND THE FIRST GLOBALIZATION OF STRUGGLES (1955–1980)

The governments and peoples of Asia and Africa proclaimed at Bandung in 1955 their desire to reconstruct the world system on the basis of the recognition of the rights of nations that until then had been dominated. This right to development was the foundation for a pattern of globalization, realized through multipolar negotiations, which compelled imperialism to adjust itself to the new demands. The success of Bandung—and not its failure, as is often said with little thought—is what produced an enormous leap forward for the peoples of the South in the areas of education and health, the formation of modern states and the reduction of social inequality, and the move into industrialization. Undoubtedly, the limits of these achievements, in particular the lack of democracy in the regimes of national populism, which "gave to the people" but never allowed them to organize themselves, must be taken into serious consideration in drawing up a balance sheet of the era.

The Bandung system was linked to two other systems that characterized the postwar era, the Soviet (and Maoist) system and the welfare state of Western social democracy. The systems were in competition, in conflict even, but they were also complementary. In this situation, it makes sense to speak of the globalization of struggles. For the first time in the history of capitalism, struggles took place in every region of the planet and within every nation, inaugurating a change in the direction of capitalism's evolution.

Proof of the interdependence characterizing the struggles and the historic compromises that maintained stability in the societies in question was provided by the course of events that followed the parallel erosion of the potential of all three systems. The collapse of the Soviet system also entailed the collapse of the social democratic model, whose social advances, entirely real, were brought about because they were the only means possible to oppose the "communist challenge." The echo of the Chinese Cultural Revolution in Europe in 1968 should also be remembered in this regard.

The progress of industrialization begun during the Bandung era did not proceed from the logic of imperialist expansion, but was imposed through the victories of the peoples of the South. Undoubtedly, this progress fed the illusion of "catching up," which appeared to be happening, while imperialism, forced to adjust to the demands for development of the peripheries, restructured itself around new forms of domination. The old contrast between the imperialist countries and the dominated countries, which was synonymous with the contrast between the industrialized and the non-industrialized countries, gave way, little by little, to a new contrast founded on the centralization of the advantages associated with the five new monopolies of the imperialist centers: the control of new technologies, natural resources, flows of financial capital, communications and information, and weapons of mass destruction. I am referring here to the interpretation of the period following the Second World War that I advanced in *Obsolescent Capitalism*.[3]

The achievements of the period, as well as the limitations, lead us to return to the central question of the future of the bourgeoisie and capitalism in the peripheries of the system. This is an enduring question insofar as the global unfolding of capitalism, as a result of the polarizing effects produced by imperialism, leads to a basic inequality between the centers and the peripheries with respect to the potential for bourgeois and capitalist development. In other words, is the bourgeoisie of the peripheries necessarily forced to submit to the requirements of this unequal development? Is it necessarily a comprador bourgeoisie? Is the capitalist path, in these conditions, necessarily a dead end? Or does the margin of maneuver from which the bourgeoisie can benefit in certain circumstances (which would have to be specified) allow for a national and autonomous capitalist development capable of "catching up"? What are the limits to these possibilities? At what point does the existence of limits force us to describe the capitalist path as illusory?

Doctrinaire and one-sided responses have been brought to these questions, adapted *ex post facto* to developments that had never been correctly predicted by either the dominant forces or the popular classes. In the aftermath of the Second World War, the communists of the Third International described all the bourgeoisies of the South as comprador, and Maoism proclaimed that the only possible path to liberation was the one opened by a socialist revolution which proceeded in stages, led by the proletariat and its allies (the peasant classes in particular) and, above all, by their vanguard representative, the Communist Party. Bandung set out to prove that this judgment was hasty and that under the leadership of the bourgeoisie a hegemonic national populist bloc could advance development. I was personally involved in these early debates, prior to Bandung, in the pages of the journal *Moyen Orient* in 1950 and 1951, taking a position in favor of "positive neutralism," which prepared the way for Bandung.[4] The Bandung era was brought to a close by the neoliberal offensive of the oligopolies of the imperialist center (the triad: the United States, Europe, Japan). Beginning in 1980, the bourgeoisies of the South again appeared in a subordinate comprador position, as expressed by the imposition of unilateral adjustments (this adjustment of the peripheries to the demands of the centers is, in some ways, the inverse of the adjustment of the centers to the peripheries during the Bandung era). But hardly had this reversal appeared, when, again, in the so-called emerging countries (particularly China, but also other countries such as India and Brazil) a new window of opportunity opened, offering the possibility for national capitalist development. Without a deepened analysis of these potential advances and their contradictions and limits it will not be possible to construct effective strategies for the convergence of local and international struggles.

THE TRAGEDY OF THE GREAT REVOLUTIONS

The "great revolutions" are distinguished by the fact that they project themselves far in front of the present, toward the future, in opposition to others (the "ordinary revolutions"), which are content to respond to the necessity for transformations that are on the agenda of the moment.

There have been only three great revolutions in the modern era—the French, Russian, and Chinese. The French revolution was not only a "bourgeois revolution," replacing the *Ancien Régime* with the capitalist order and the aristocracy with bourgeois power, it was just as much a popular revolution (and particularly a peasant one) whose demands called the bourgeois order into question. The democratic and radically secular Republic, whose ideal was the distribution of small property to everyone, did not proceed from the simple logic of the accumulation of capital (founded on inequality) but denied it (and proclaimed its consciousness of this by declaring economic liberalism to be the enemy of democracy). In this sense, the French Revolution already contained the germ of the socialist revolutions to come, whose objective conditions were obviously not present in France at that time (the Babouvists are evidence of that). The Russian and Chinese Revolutions (with which the revolutions in Vietnam and Cuba may be associated) also assigned themselves the goal of communism well in advance of the objective requirements for the solution of the immediate problems of the societies concerned.

Great revolutions suffer from the repercussions of being in advance of their time. Retreats and reactionary restorations follow the brief moments of their radicalization. These revolutions, then, always experience great difficulty in becoming stabilized (the stabilization of the French revolution took a century). In contrast, other revolutions begin the stable and calm development of the system. For example, the English and American revolutions were content to take note of the requirements of the social and political relations already present within the framework of nascent capitalism. Consequently, these "revolutions" hardly merit the name, so marked were their compromises with the forces of the past and their absence of a vision of the future.

Despite their failures, great revolutions make history—in the long run. Through the avant-garde values that define their project, they make it possible for creative utopian ideas to win over minds and, eventually, achieve the supreme ambition of modernity, which is to make human beings the active subjects of their own history. These values contrast with those of the bourgeois order, which promote behaviors of passive adjustment to the so-called objective requirements of capitalist development and give complete power to the economic alienation that underlies this submission.

THE FORCE OF IMPERIALISM: A PERMANENT STAGE IN THE WORLDWIDE EXPANSION OF CAPITALISM

The worldwide development of capitalism has always been polarizing, from the beginning and at each stage of its history. This characteristic of capitalism, however essential, has always been underestimated, to say the least, because of the Eurocentrism that dominates modern thought, including the ideological formulations of the vanguards in the great revolutions. Historical Marxism, in the successive Internationals, only partially escaped this general rule.

To understand the immense significance of imperialist reality and the strategic consequences concerning the transformation of the world that it implies is the primary imperative for the social and political forces of the victims of capitalist development, both in the centers and in the peripheries. Imperialism has placed on the agenda not so much the maturation of conditions leading to socialist revolutions (or an increase in developments moving in that direction) but challenges to its order from revolts in its peripheries. Thus, it is not by accident that Russia in 1917 was the "weak link" in the system or that revolution in the name of socialism moved afterward toward the East (China, among others) while the expectation of a collapse in the West, in which Lenin placed his hopes, was disappointed. Consequently, the revolutionized societies in question were confronted with the contradictory task of "catching up" (which implies the use of methods analogous to those of capitalism) and "doing something else" (constructing socialism). The combination of these tasks was, here or there, what it was. Maybe it could have been better, in the sense that it could have allowed for the progressive strengthening of communist aspirations along with efforts at "catching up." It is always the case that this contradiction is at the center of the objective conditions for the historical evolution of post-revolutionary societies.

The forms of organization and political action invented in these circumstances by the revolutionary parties—the communists of the Third International—were circumscribed by the idea that the movement itself made the revolution, which was considered to be imminent since all of its objective conditions were thought to be present together. The party, then, had to make up for what alone was lacking: the creation of an organization charged with making the revolution, which implied, in the circumstances, that the accent was placed on homogeneity and quasi-military discipline. The parties in question retained these organizational forms even though the prospect of an immediate revolutionary assault had been abandoned since the end of the 1920s. They were then put in the service of a totally different objective: defense of the Soviet state, from within as well as from outside. The dissolution of the Comintern in 1943 proceeded from this same logic.

In the peripheries of global capitalism, by definition zones of instability within the imperialist system, a form of revolution remained on the agenda. But its objective remained ambiguous and vague: national liberation from imperialism—and preservation of the social relations of capitalist modernity—or might there be room for something more? Whether it was a question of the radical revolutions in China, Vietnam and Cuba or of others elsewhere in Asia, Africa, and Latin America, the challenge remained: "catch up" or "do something else." This challenge was connected, in turn, with another task also considered to be a priority: defense of an encircled Soviet Union.

THE DEFENSE OF POST-REVOLUTIONARY STATES THROUGH VANGUARD STRATEGIES

The Soviet Union and later China were confronted with a systematic attempt by the Western powers to isolate them. It is noteworthy that, during one-third of the brief history of the United States, the strategy of this hegemonic power of the capitalist system was organized around the objective of destroying its two opponents, regardless of whether they were truly socialist or not. Washington succeeded both in involving and subordinating its allies to this strategy. This was true of the other centers of the triad (Europe and Japan) as well as the peripheries, where the power of comprador classes was progressively substituted for populist-oriented power arising out of national liberation movements.

Since revolution was not, in the immediate future, on the agenda elsewhere in the world, it is possible, then, to understand that priority was generally given to safeguarding post-revolutionary states. The political strategies implemented by Lenin and then by Stalin and his successors in the Soviet Union, and those implemented in Maoist and post-Maoist China, as well as those embraced by the national populist states in Asia and Africa and those proposed by the communist vanguards (regardless of whether they followed Moscow or Peking or were independent), were all defined in relation to the central task of defending post-revolutionary states.

The Soviet Union and China both experienced the vicissitudes of great revolutions and were confronted by the consequences of the unequal expansion of global capitalism. Both gradually sacrificed their original communist objectives to the immediate requirements of "catching up" economically. This shift, abandoning the objective of social property—which is how Marx defined communism—and substituting state management, accompanied by the decline of popular democracy, prepared the way for the quick evolution toward the restoration of capitalism common to both experiences, despite the different paths followed. In both experiences, priority was given to defense of the post-revolutionary state, and the internal means used for this purpose were accompanied by external strategies that prioritized this defense. Communist parties were asked to align themselves with these choices, not only in their general strategic orientation but also in their day-to-day tactical adjustments. That could produce nothing other than a rapid weakening of the critical thinking of revolutionaries whose abstract discourse on revolution (always imminent) moved away from analysis of the real contradictions of society, supported by the preservation of quasi-military forms of organization.

The vanguard countries that refused to align themselves with this strategy, and sometimes dared to face up to the realities of the post-revolutionary societies, nevertheless did not renounce the original Leninist hypothesis (imminent revolution), ignoring that the latter's possibility was more and more visibly contradicted by reality. This was true of Trotskyism and the parties of the Fourth International. It was true of a large number of revolutionary organizations inspired by Maoism or Guevarism.[5] Examples are numerous, from the Philippines to India (the Naxalites),[6] from the Arab world (with the Qawmiyin movement and its emulators in South Yemen)[7] to Latin America.

NATIONAL AND SOCIALIST CONSTRUCTION IN THE RADICALIZED PERIPHERIES

The main national liberation movements in Asia and Africa, which entered into open conflict with the imperialist order, came up against the conflicting demands of "catching up" (national construction) and the transformation of social relations in favor of the popular classes, just as the socialist revolutions did. The post-revolutionary (or simply post-independence) regimes were certainly less radical than the communist powers about transforming social relations. This is why I describe these regimes in Asia and Africa as "national-populist." These regimes were sometimes inspired by forms of organization (the single party, undemocratic dictatorship, state management of the economy) developed in the experiences of "really existing socialism." They generally diluted the effectiveness of these organizational forms with vague ideological choices and compromises with the past.

In these conditions, the regimes at the time, just like the vanguard parties (historical communism in the countries concerned), were asked to support the Soviet Union (more rarely China) and benefit from its support. The formation of this united front against the imperialist aggression of the United States and its European and Japanese partners was beneficial for the peoples of Asia and Africa. This anti-imperialist front opened up a degree of autonomy both for the initiatives of the ruling classes of the countries concerned and for the action of their popular classes. Proof of that is provided by what happened after the Soviet collapse. Even before that, the ruling classes who opted for the West (viz. Anwar El Sadat) nourished the illusion that this turnabout would be favorable. (In the Egyptian case, it was thought that the United States held 90 percent of the cards in the Palestinian question and that their friendship would make it possible to turn the situation in favor of the Arab and Palestinian cause.) In the end, nothing was gained. On the contrary, capitulation favored the implementation of offensive strategies by imperialism (and, in the Egyptian circumstances, reinforced the Washington-Tel Aviv axis).

The conditions that the Soviet Union imposed on the political forces that were supporting the popular classes in allied countries (and particularly on the Communist parties) remain questionable. One would suppose that within this anti-imperialist front the parties would retain complete autonomy of movement, consequently recognizing the conflicting interests and social projects of the partners associated in the front. Within this context, the ruling classes definitely pursued a capitalist project, although "national" in nature. However, satisfying the interests of the popular classes required going beyond this perspective. Subsequent history has clearly demonstrated the narrow limits of the national capitalist project. On the other hand, the choices of the Soviet state nourished the inherent illusions of this project, consequently weakening autonomous action by the popular classes. The invention of the alleged non-capitalist path expressed this choice.

Undoubtedly, during this period of the Bandung era, it was difficult to make a distinction between the interests of the ruling authorities and those of their peoples. These authorities were newly emerged from large liberation movements that had defeated imperialism in its old forms (colonial and semi-colonial). Sometimes they had emerged from true revolutions made by these movements (China, Vietnam, Cuba). They were, thus, close to their peoples and benefited from strong legitimacy.

The great majority of Arab communists, just like communists elsewhere, accepted the recommendation of the Soviet leadership to become, at best, the leftwing of the national-populist and anti-imperialist regimes. In other words, offer barely critical, practically unconditional support. The self-dissolution of the Egyptian Communist Party in 1965, in the illusory hope of being able to revive the Nasserist Socialist Party, and the rallying of Khaled Bakdash[8] to the thesis that national construction was the only item on the agenda are examples of this choice. I have commented on this important question elsewhere, particularly on the occasion of the publication in Egypt of the memoirs of numerous militants of the period. My conclusion was that Arab communism, as a whole, had not moved outside of the essential context of the national-populist project, ignoring that the latter was ultimately part of a strictly capitalist perspective. This choice was not conjunctural and opportunist. It was structural and reflected the original shortcomings of these communist movements, the ambiguity of the ideologies they supported and, in the end, their ignorance of the popular classes whose immediate and long-term social interests they were supposed to defend. The result of this unfortunate choice was that the communists lost their credibility as soon as the national-populist regimes, having attained their historical limits, began to see their legitimacy eroded. Since the communist Left was not posed as an alternative to national-populism, a political vacuum was created, opening the way for the disastrous entry of political Islam on the scene.

No doubt some Arab communists refused to rally unconditionally to the defense of the Soviet state. The examples of the Qawmiyin and their emulators in South Yemen and several small Maoist groups testify to this. But they did not move beyond the limits of the originally Leninist hypothesis that the revolution was imminent. In this way, they shared the view of the Guevarists in Latin America and the Naxalites in India. The defeat of the courageous movements that they inspired demonstrates, *a posteriori*, that the Leninist thesis proceeded from tragic simplifications and was ultimately erroneous.

MAOISM'S CONTRIBUTION

The Marxism of the Second International, workerist and Eurocentric, shared with the dominant ideology of the era a linear view of historical progress in which every society must pass first through a stage of capitalist development before being able to aspire to socialism. The idea that the "development" of some societies (the dominant centers) and the "underdevelopment" of others (the dominated peripheries) is an immanent product of the worldwide expansion of capitalism was completely alien.

Understanding the polarization inherent in capitalist globalization is essential for formulating any view about transcending capitalism. This polarization lies behind the possible rallying of large fractions of the popular classes and above all the middle classes (whose development is itself favored by the position of the centers in the world system) of the dominant countries to social-colonialism. At the same time, it transforms the peripheries into a *zone des tempêtes*, in a continual natural rebellion against the capitalist world order. Certainly rebellion is not synonymous with revolution, but only with the possibility of revolution. On the other hand, grounds for rejecting the capitalist model are not lacking in the center of the system, as 1968, among other things, illustrated. Undoubtedly, the formulation of the challenge by the Communist Party of China (CPC), at a given moment, in terms of the countryside encircling the cities, is too extreme to be useful. A global strategy of transition beyond capitalism in the direction of world socialism must articulate the struggles in both the centers and peripheries of the system.

Initially, Lenin kept some distance from the dominant theory of the Second International and successfully led a revolution in the "weak link" (Russia), though always with the conviction that this would be followed by a wave of socialist revolutions in Europe. This was a disappointed hope. Lenin then formulated a view that stressed transforming rebellions in the East into revolutions. The CPC and Mao would systematize this new perspective.

The Russian Revolution had been led by a party firmly entrenched in the working class and radical intelligentsia. Its alliance with the peasantry (represented by the Socialist-Revolutionary Party) was naturally vital. The radical agrarian reform that resulted finally satisfied an old dream of the Russian peasantry: to become property owners. But this historical compromise carried the seeds of its own demise: the market produced on its own, as always, growing differentiation within the peasantry (the well-known phenomenon of "kulakization").

The Chinese Revolution set out from the beginning (or at least from the 1930s) on bases that guaranteed a solid alliance with the poor and middle peasantry. Moreover, the national dimension, the war of resistance against Japanese aggression, also made it possible for the communists to recruit widely from the bourgeois classes that were disappointed by the weaknesses and betrayals of the Koumintang. The Chinese Revolution consequently produced a new situation, different from that of post-revolutionary Russia. The radical peasant revolution did away with the idea of private property in agrarian land and substituted a guarantee for all peasants of equal access to the land. Up till now this decisive advantage, which is common to no other country except Vietnam, is the major obstacle to a devastating expansion of agrarian capitalism. The debates underway in China revolve, in great part, around this question.[9] But the rallying of numerous bourgeois nationalists to the Communist Party should have an ideological influence that is favorable to supporting the deviations of those whom Mao called "capitalist roaders."

The post-revolutionary regime in China has to its credit a good many political, cultural, material, and economic achievements (industrialization of the country, radicalization of its modern political culture, etc.). Maoist China also resolved the "peasant problem" that lay at the center of the decline of the Middle Kingdom during two decisive centuries, 1750–1950, as described in my work *The Future of Maoism*.[10] Moreover, Maoist China succeeded in achieving these results by avoiding the most tragic excesses of the Soviet Union: collectivization was not imposed by murderous violence, as was the case with Stalinism; opposition within the Party did not give rise to the institution of terror (Deng Xiaoping was removed, he returned). The objective of relative equality involving not only the distribution of income among peasants and workers but also between them and the ruling strata was pursued tenaciously, with ups and downs. It was formalized in development strategies that clearly contrast with those of the USSR (these choices were formulated in ten great reports at the beginning of the 1960s). It was these successes that account for post-Maoist China's extraordinary growth beginning in the 1980s. The contrast with India, which has not had a revolution, assumes its full significance here, not only in accounting for the different paths followed during the decades 1950 to 1980 but also for probable future prospects. It is these successes that explain why post-Maoist China, henceforth incorporating its development into the new capitalist globalization has not suffered from destructive shocks similar to those that followed the collapse of the USSR.

The successes of Maoism have not, for all that, definitively settled the question of the long-term prospects for socialism. The development strategy of 1950–1980 had exhausted its potential and, among other things, an opening (albeit controlled) was imperative.[11] As the result demonstrated, this involved the risk of reinforcing the tendencies of an evolution in a capitalist direction. Simultaneously, the system of Maoist China combined contradictory tendencies that both strengthened and weakened socialist options.

Conscious of this contradiction, Mao attempted to bend the stick in favor of socialism through the Cultural Revolution (1966 to 1974). An appeal went out to "bombard the headquarters" (the Party's Central Committee), seat of the bourgeois aspirations of the political class. Mao believed that, to undertake this course of correction, he could rely on the youth (who, among other things, greatly inspired the 1968 events in Europe; see Jean-Luc Godard's film *La Chinoise*). The result of these events demonstrated the error of this judgment. The Cultural Revolution came to a close; the partisans of the capitalist path were encouraged to go on the offensive.

The struggle between the long and difficult socialist path and the capitalist option is certainly not over for good. The conflict between capitalism and socialism is the real "clash of civilizations" of our time. In this struggle, the Chinese people have some significant assets, which are the heritage of the revolution and of Maoism. These assets exist in various spheres of social life. They are forcefully apparent in the peasantry's defense of state ownership of agricultural land and guaranteed access to it for all.

Maoism contributed decisively to making an accurate assessment of the issues and the challenges represented by global capitalist expansion. It allowed us to bring into focus the challenge of the contrast between the center and the periphery immanent to the expansion of capitalism, and then to draw all the lessons that this implies for the socialist struggle, in the dominant centers as well as the dominated peripheries. These conclusions have been summarized in a wonderful Chinese-style phrase: "Countries want independence, nations want liberation, and the people want revolution." Countries, that is, the ruling classes of countries, when they are something other than lackeys, intermediaries for outside forces, devote themselves to enlarging their space for movement. This enables them to maneuver in the world system and raise themselves to the position of active participants in the shaping of the world order. Nations, that is, historical blocs of potentially progressive classes, want liberation, development and modernization. People, that is, the dominated and exploited classes, aspire to socialism. The phrase allows us to understand the real world in all its complexity and therefore formulate effective strategies for action. It is part of the viewpoint that it is a long—very long—transition from capitalism to world socialism, which breaks with the short transition concept of the Third International.

CHAPTER TWO

NEW ERA, NEW CHALLENGES

The three dominant systems of the period following the Second World War have ceased to exist, opening the way to the triumphant offensive of capital. Capitalism and imperialism have entered into a new phase in their development, bearing qualitatively new characteristics. The identification of these transformations and their real significance must be placed at the center of our discussions. Important work on these questions is not lacking.

I have put forward some central theses on these transformations that are useful to recall here:

1. Transformations in the organization of work and in the stratification of social classes and groups in relation to the technological revolution underway (information, genetic, space, and nuclear), as well as accelerated industrialization in the emergent peripheries have generated a complex set of social and political actors, with a new articulation of possible conflicts and alliances. The precise identification of these new subjects of social transformation—their interests and aspirations, their views of the challenges, and the conflicts that separate them and create obstacles to their convergence in diversity—is the first condition for a fruitful debate on strategy for local and global struggles.

2. The dichotomy between the center and the periphery is no longer synonymous with the dichotomy between the industrialized countries and the non-industrialized countries. The polarization between the center and the periphery, which gives global capitalist expansion its imperialist character, is continuing, and is

even being deepened, through the five new monopolies enjoyed by the imperialist centers. In these conditions, the continuation of the development projects of the emergent peripheries, implemented with unquestionable immediate success (particularly in China, but also in other countries of the South) cannot to abolish imperialist domination. This particular development contributes to the formation of a new dichotomy between the center and the periphery, but does not transcend it.

3. The noun imperialism is no longer to be conjugated in the plural as in previous historical periods. From now on, it is a collective imperialism of the triad of the United States, Europe, and Japan. In this sense, the common interests that the oligopolies based in the triad share will prevail over their (commercial) conflicts of interest. This collective character of imperialism is expressed through the management of the world system by the triad's common instruments. On the economic plane, there is the WTO (the triad's Ministry of Colonies), the IMF (the collective Colonial Monetary Agency), the World Bank (Ministry of Propaganda), and the OECD and the European Union (set up to prevent Europe from abandoning liberalism). On the political plane, there is the G7/G8, the armed forces of the United States, and NATO. The marginalization and domestication of the United Nations completes the picture.

4. The hegemonic project of the United States is implemented through a program for military control of the planet, entailing, among other things, the abrogation of international law and Washington's self-proclaimed right to wage preventive wars whenever it wishes. It is organized around the new collective imperialism and gives the American leadership the means to compensate for the economic deficiencies of the United States.

Other studies of the current transformations of capitalism have been carried out. I believe it is necessary to indicate, briefly. the broad outlines of the conclusions that they have reached·

1. A current idea is that the scientific revolution underway entails the abolition of forms of labor subject to vertical hierarchies of command and substitutes a networked organization of

free individuals. In this new mode of production, founded on the domination of science, the individual would become the true subject of history, taking over the tasks of the historical subjects characteristic of earlier phases such as classes or nations.

2. Another idea put forward, no doubt complementary to the preceding one, is that the era of imperialism has been surpassed and that in the current system of post-imperialist globalization the center is everywhere and nowhere. The confrontation of multiple and fragmented economic and social powers has taken the place of confrontation between states, formerly the site where the power of relatively stable hegemonic blocs was crystallized.

3. Emphasis is placed on the "financialization" of the management of the new patrimonial capitalism, which is not analyzed as a set of conjunctural phenomena particular to the present moment of transition (a transition that leads to a new system, whose nature is, moreover, itself subject to debate), but precisely as stable characteristics of the new system under construction.

I will not hide that I have serious reservations with regard to these theses.[12] What I propose to do in what follows is to make some observations concerning a desirable political method, so that these debates may be of service in the positive construction of an alternative based on the principle of convergence in diversity.

OBSOLESCENT CAPITALISM, ENEMY OF THE HUMAN RACE

The project of global liberalism imagines that it is possible and desirable to have the management of society reduced to that of a market economy freed of all constraints. This would be possible because the deregulated market would produce a stable equilibrium of supply and demand and desirable, moreover, because this general equilibrium would be effective (promoting the quickest innovative dynamic) and socially optimal (all classes would benefit from the general progress). Conventional economic thought, regardless of the growing complexity of its formulations, has never gone beyond this infantile view, which has no relation to reality or the demands of scientific rigor. This is an ideology, in the most vulgar sense of the word. It is an ideology that claims that this form of social management is the only "rational" one and consequently able to produce the best of all possible worlds. In this sense, the liberalism implemented at the current moment is only the expression of the permanent utopia of capital, the dream of a world submitting completely and exclusively to the unilateral requirements of financial profitability. This utopia is not viable. It can only produce the chaos that is the obvious result of the resistance and revolts of its victims. This ideology presupposes an apolitical economic management, reducing the state to the "night watchman" role of guaranteeing order. Real history, not the imaginary history of transhistorical economics, is produced by the complementary and conflictual relationship between the requirements of the reproduction of the economy and the state. The latter is the site where the compromises between different social interests are crystallized, some convergent, others divergent. Any compromise is historical, belonging to a given situation and given moment.

The question is not whether the neoliberal project is or is not absurd. It is absurd and not viable. But it exists. The question is why it has asserted itself with such force. The success of a group of retrograde conceptions was possible only because the systems that managed the world's societies in the preceding historical stage exhausted their own potential. I am referring here to the three postwar social models (the Welfare State, the Soviet system, and national-populism). The collapse of these three models has produced the opportunity for a total submission of society to the unilateral demands of capital and given rise to confusion in the victims of the new order, since their reference points have lost credibility and legitimacy. This disequilibrium, which is to the sole benefit of capital, finds its confirmation in the naïve invitation made to the victims to accept their fate. "Workers must understand that it is necessary to accept a reduction in their wages" is the constant refrain of the experts who occupy the forefront of the media scene. Do we ever hear the contrary? "Capitalists must understand that it is necessary to accept a reduction in their profits."

In actuality, the implementation of the neoliberal project has produced what it had to produce: social regression, growing inequality and impoverishment (the discourse on "poverty" is a sort of naïve recognition of this), increasing insecurity and the anxiety that follows, loss of credibility of democratic practices (impotence of "elected" authorities), and ultimately instability and political chaos. As a counterpoint to this dominant discourse, I assert that the project implemented by all of the classes holding power at the current moment of neoliberal globalization is not viable. Capitalism has reached a stage in its development where its victim (its opponent) is no longer formed exclusively by the proletariat, whose labor it exploits, but by humanity as a whole, whose survival it threatens. I have described the system that has reached this stage as obsolescent, which, consequently, has no future other than to give way to another (possible) world. The latter could be better, but it could also be worse. In two areas, liberal capitalism (and doubtless capitalism, period) is already an obsolete system: in its relations with the peasantry (half of humanity) and in the waste of the planet's natural resources that its continual deployment entails.

The continuing accumulation of capital henceforth requires the destruction of peasant societies, which make up half of humanity, through the spread of a policy of "enclosures" on a world scale, without the system being able to employ the peasants, who have been chased from the countryside for industrial activities and profitable services. The size of the challenge posed by the increasingly rapid construction of a planet of shantytowns should not be underestimated.[13]

It also leads to the rapid exhaustion of nonrenewable resources, the accelerated destruction of biodiversity and the exacerbation of the threats that strongly affect the ecological balances that are essential for the reproduction of life on Earth. Incontestable quantified data exist which demonstrate that capitalist civilization cannot continue its destructive expansion for long. Preserving the way of life of the United States alone would lead to pillaging all of the resources of the planet for its sole benefit. The energy crisis has already produced military aggression in the Middle East. "The American way of life is not negotiable," the president of this country reminds us. In other words, the extermination of the "redskins," who hinder U.S. expansion, will be continued.

Expansion requires, in combination with the depreciation of marketable labor power, the intensification of the contribution of non-marketable labor, provided mainly by women. The continuing accumulation of capital has become an obstacle to the production of the possible wealth implicit in the development of science and technology.

This development means that the historical subject of desirable transformations must from now on be viewed in the plural. The growing number of areas of intervention for movements of resistance and protest struggles bears witness to the multiplicity of anti-capitalist historical subjects. But this multiplicity through which the power of the social is expressed is, at the same time, because of its dispersion, the manifestation of the immediate weakness of this same movement. The accumulation of demands, as legitimate as they are (and they are legitmate), and the sum of the struggles carried out in their name are not an effective alternative.

The challenge is therefore serious and will only be surmounted insofar as there will be coalitions capable of leading shared struggles to victory and constructing hegemonic blocs that are alternatives to those that exercise power within the framework of contemporary capitalism. The challenge is such that it is difficult to imagine that an effective action can be content with an immediate and partial response (which aims at giving a human face to capitalism) without being part of a perspective that aims to go beyond capitalism. Doubtless any strategy for effective struggle must know how to define short-term objectives and others of a longer-term nature, that is, identify the stages of the movement's advance. Unquestionably, affirmation of the distant objective alone (such as, for example, socialism) is not only insufficient but also runs the risk of discouraging mobilizations of militants. Objectives of immediate import must be identified and action organized with a view to ensure victories in the struggles carried out by these mobilized militants. But that is also insufficient. It is necessary more than ever to restore the legitimacy and credibility of a more distant prospect: socialism/communism.

After the collapse of the Soviet system, when China abandoned Maoism to pursue the path we all know, when the national-populist regimes that had known their glory days during the Bandung era sunk into corruption and excesses of various kinds, the term socialism lost all credible and legitimate meaning. The regimes arising from the revolutions led in the name of socialism and formed by the victorious national liberation movements—which became embroiled in shameful and sometimes criminal deviations and sunk into the lie of an empty and repetitive rhetoric—are responsible for this collapse of hope, a situation of which capital took immediate advantage.

It is not surprising in these conditions that the revived movement, during the first years of its development in the 1990s, accepted capitalism as, if not the end of history, at least as the horizon of the visible future and scorned the rights of nations that are the victim of imperialist expansion. But it is time to understand that this moment must be surpassed. It is time to understand that the savage neoliberal offensive only reveals the true face of capitalism and imperialism.

THE EMERGENCE OF THE WORLD SOCIAL FORUM

It is this particular set of circumstances that lies behind the explosion of social movements and the great variety in forms of organization and expression in the present period. The collapse of the political ideologies around which the supporters of the three post-war models of social reproduction were organized and the movements associated with them has certainly contributed to more confusion. If, from a certain point of view, one can say that all (or almost all) of the movements are expressions of protest, this is not to say that this "protest" is always directed against those responsible for the disaster.

The movement has already won a moral victory. "The World is Not for Sale" and "Another World is Possible" are not empty slogans. They are battle cries that have already conquered the sympathy of public opinion throughout the world.

The movement in question is multiple, this is precisely its strength, even if this makes it more difficult to unite around and prioritize strategic objectives. Winning significant battles on precise points, on the national, regional, and world levels, is the only means to achieve irreversible advances in the struggle for a new world. That entails in-depth and systematic discussion of the choice of objectives and the organization of suitable campaigns of action.

This multiplicity lies first of all in the objectives and, behind them, in the social interests of classes. The movement is mobilizing important segments of the educated middle classes, above all in countries in the center of the system. Such organizations are always focused on a single objective (the advancement of women, respect for the environment, defense of cultural and other oppressed minorities, progress of rights, etc.). These organizations are built for the long run or for a particular battle. They are often inter-class on principle. It is pleasing to see this positive transformation in the political activities of social strata that were often content to use their right to vote and the other means of representative democracy (lobbies, working through political parties and elected officials). The defense of the individual (and the freedom of individual initiative) and the strong moral dimension characteristic of many of these movements are not "petty bourgeois deviations," as a certain tradition in the workers' movement often considered them, but progress in political practice to the benefit of all dominated classes.

The fact remains, however, that these new movements have not led to the disappearance of working class movements struggling for so-called material interests. Workers' struggles for employment, wages, and job security, and peasant struggles for remunerative prices, access to the land and means to cultivate it properly, and agrarian reforms will continue to form the central axis of struggles likely to change the social balance of power. Unions and peasant organizations, consequently, are essential organizations for the movement. That is not always accepted because the middle classes often occupy the forefront in movement meetings. Unquestionably, the classic organizations through which the dominated classes express themselves and act are far from being appropriate to the new challenges. Transformations in the organization of labor and the management of economic life produced by the evolution of capitalism call for forms of organization and struggle by workers' and peasants' movements, such as those that make up, among other things, the working program of the World Forum for Alternatives. But these transformations do not justify the contempt that many other movements hold for so-called traditional unions and peasant organizations.

The principal threat confronting the movement is the risk of naïvely believing that it is possible to "change the world without taking power." It remains true that powerful social movements have succeeded at certain moments in history in changing society without taking state power. The year 1968 changed many things (in the West) and did so positively: the rapid development of feminist demands and increased individual democratic responsibility should count as gains. Yet, capitalism demonstrated that it was capable of absorbing these changes without calling into question its fundamental modes of exploitation and oppression. Today, some postmodern thinkers and others lend legitimacy to what amounts to a call to do nothing with the idea that revolutionary transformation happens spontaneously.

At the same time, debate is crucial on what is required for the progress of social movements and for changing the social balance of power. There is not a shadow of doubt that this entails the invention of "another way of doing politics." But the proposal thus formulated is too vague to be anything other than empty.

THE NECESSITY OF QUESTIONING THE CONCEPT OF DIVERSITY

Diversity of "social movements" is not a characteristic unique to our era but is the rule across history, at least modern history. The trajectory of history is the product of transformations in the social balance of power caused by the struggles carried out by these movements and the conflicts among them. This general formulation of the place of social movements in history should be considered a platitude, obviously without any great significance in itself. Further, to speak of social movements without specifying the nature of their objectives, their terrain of struggle, and their choice of alliances is meaningless. This commonsense observation would not even merit attention if it were not that, in the current moment, the "diversity" of movements is sometimes asserted as a fundamental value, positive in itself, and as a consequence it is prohibited to make any judgment whatsoever concerning any movement. Since any movement has the right to exist, it consequently evades any obligation to listen to the assessment that others make of it. This formulation does away with confrontation and debate and rejects doing politics (an option condemned from the beginning, moreover). Each movement has its own strategy, its own objectives. That is its right (obviously). However, more is inferred from that: any search for shared collective strategies, for broad alliances of diverse movements would not only be useless (history does not need such pretentiousness to advance), but also dangerous for fundamental human liberties (the anti-totalitarian discourse has a wonderful time with this type of critique of the political). Can this position be described as absolute libertarianism? Yes, if one wants to do so.

The analysis that I offer strives to be a contribution to the fundamental political debate of our time: how to construct a convergence in diversity that will make it possible for dominated and oppressed classes and peoples to advance. With whom should this unity be built? What movements can, by rallying around common objectives, make it possible to move in this direction? Such a debate is necessarily political (rejecting the idea that movements can be allowed to evolve according to the particular logic that governs their existence) and necessarily concrete (particular to a specific situation, characterizing a country or a region at a given moment).

LIMITS AND AMBIGUITIES OF SOCIAL MOVEMENTS

Progressive and Reactionary Social Movements

There have always been progressive social movements and reactionary ones (the fascist movements are proof of the latter). The nature of the classes and segments of society in which one type of movement or the other recruit or encounters the most favorable echoes is not in itself a criterion guaranteeing the progressive or reactionary character of movements. Some movements, moreover, do not always visibly serve definite social interests. Many are active in areas, such as religion, that appear to be quite distant from the terrain on which economic and social interests confront one another.

In order to understand how all social movements are participants in social conflicts and understand what interests they serve, it is not possible to dispense with detailed analyses and criteria for judgment that only have meaning in relation to the viewpoint of a plan for the society that one is attempting to promote. Thus, I will propose criteria that respond to the issues in social conflicts and that are suitable for debates concerning strategies for building progressive alliances.

The criterion is simple: a movement can only meaningfully be described as progressive if it contributes unhesitatingly to the support of struggles working for social progress. This requires that the policies of economic growth or development it supports be based on social objectives, such as employment, increase in workers' incomes, implementation of effective public services for everyone, etc. But I add that the objectives of social progress in question must be achieved by the implementation and strengthening of democratic methods of social management. This additional condition thus excludes movements that are overtly anti-democratic, entrusting the future to so-called charismatic individuals. I also add a second condition concerning the national context of the struggle. A movement that would sacrifice social and democratic advances under the pretext that they must be achieved in an organized space that goes beyond the nation strongly risks, given the structure of the contemporary world, being constrained to postpone action that could be successfully undertaken within the time frame of the visible future. This position obviously poses a problem for all those who have chosen to subject local struggles to priorities defined in the European theater.

On this basis, a census of the progressive movements in the huge conglomeration known as the World Social Forum probably allows us to put the majority of the movements, given the extent of their presence in the field, in the camp of progressive forces to various degrees. All movements that defend interests threatened by neoliberalism (unions, among others), all citizen organizations dedicated to defending general or specific rights (of women, immigrants, ecology, etc.) find their place in this conception, whether these movements be radical or reformist, perhaps even moderate.

Simultaneously, a coherent structure for all three dimensions of the response to the challenge (combining as inseparable elements social progress, increasing democratization, and respect for national autonomy in a negotiated globalization) would be to require a movement to become what I would like to see materialized in a party that could respond to the challenge of our era. I will not add any superfluous and destructive description such as a (self-proclaimed) vanguard party. I imagine, rather, a (small) group of parties of this type.

Movements, including progressive ones, want to maintain their independence. This is obviously not only their right, but it is desirable because independence is precisely the origin of the effectiveness of their actions. Such independence in no way excludes the crystallization of new left parties that propose to integrate the different dimensions of responses to the challenge in a strategy of building a coherent alternative. Although there is no contradiction between these two propositions, the prospect of a revival of partisan organizations frightens some actors in the World Social Forum. The expressed fear is that this development would sound the death knell of the Forums. On the contrary, the formation of new parties can only strengthen the forces of progressive social transformation even more. Further, the stagnation of the Forums, by a supposedly apolitical form, is the best means of eliminating their potential effectiveness.

As a counterpoint to building the movements that are part of this progressive perspective, it is necessary that we identify the means, subjects, and terrains of struggle chosen by the opponent. In principle, the opponent (i.e., large transnational capital dominant in the system of neoliberalism) chooses to avoid the terrain of the concrete struggles of the working class and dominated classes in order to substitute other terrains of confrontation. This clever strategic option, perhaps, has been thought up in think tanks in the service of Washington or Brussels. I do not exclude this possibility, without for all that subscribing to a conspiratorial conception of history. But the choice in question only works because of numerous intermediaries, i.e., social movements, that respond to the challenge in this manner.

The range of movements that I will describe right away as reactionary are those that avoid the terrain of real social confrontations and will easily illustrate my meaning. At the center of the imperialist system, the neocons (and the citizens organized by them into social movements that count their members in the tens of millions) and the sects (with their televangelists) are the model of large, reactionary social movements. These movements do not pose a problem because, quite simply, they flaunt their objectives: defend Washington's imperialism, defend private property, and, at the same time, defend positions generally considered appalling in the Social Forums (homophobia, for example). Yet, these movements do not see themselves as devoted servants of large capital. They reach that conclusion because of their hostility to monopoly. The joke would go no further (an old and well-known practice of the state) were it still not a golden opportunity to gain millions of "electors"!

The true tragedy begins when such nonsense takes hold of the people who are dominated and exploited by really existing capitalism. Religious fundamentalisms, e.g., political Islam, Hinduism, Buddhism, provide the bulk of these armies of reactionary social movements. Despite the apparent variety of the movements and parties that claim one of these labels—which makes it possible for political pundits and Western political leaders to maneuver and navigate between those they condemn as terrorists and those that they accept as moderates—all these movements share fundamental points of view that place them in the camp of reactionary forces, providing support for the neoliberal project. I offer in Appendix 1 a more specific analysis of political Islam and the challenges created by the aggression of the United States against the peoples of the Middle East. The importance of the region, central to the implementation of Washington's project for military control of the planet, justifies this particular attention.

I have not described political Islam as reactionary because it is a religious movement (which, by the way, it is not). It belongs to that vulgar family of political organizations that use the mobilization of religious membership for their own ends (like Polish idolatry of the Pope, for example). By contrast, there are authentically religious movements that are resolutely progressive. Liberation theology is the best living proof of that and the movements it inspires are unhesitatingly involved in struggle alongside the working class. An "Islamist left" of the same kind is not impossible to imagine. But, quite simply, it does not exist. The embryo of the "*Fiqh al-tahrir*" (the Arabic expression synonymous with liberation theology) that Mahmoud Taha attempted to express was nipped in the bud (and Taha hanged) by the Islamists themselves, without the least protest from any tendency that claims adherence to Islam.

The considerations concerning political Islam offered here are probably valid, with appropriate alteration of details, for political Hinduism or Buddhism. In India, the pro-liberal and comprador Right gains support from the declining Congress Party and political Hinduism. The ravings of the Dalai Lama, moreover, mobilized by the Bush clique into the camp of Good against the Devil (the Chinese, to be specific), are treated with the greatest benevolence by many progressive organizations.

Socially reactionary movements do not parade only under a religious disguise. There are just as many movements that organize behind the tawdry appearance of a fabricated ethnic authenticity. Croats, Bosnian Muslims, Kosovars, and Baltic peoples define themselves in that way, just like others, particularly in Africa. They substitute belonging to tribal, ethnic, or para-ethnic communities for belonging to the nations formed in the aftermath of the victory of national liberation struggles. All these "nationalisms" are not really nationalist, in the sense that they are not asserting themselves in response to the challenge of liberal globalization under the leadership of the United States. On the contrary, they are part of the camp of those who unconditionally support all the initiatives of transnational capital and the armed diplomacy of Washington and NATO. Their "nationalism" is asserted only against their neighbors and, as such, is put in the service of the imperialist strategy of weakening peoples by increasing their internal divisions. Supporting these "claims" under the pretext that the regimes against which their authors are rebelling have mismanaged the diversity in question (and this accusation is, at least to a certain extent, almost always true) certainly is of no help in getting out of the impasse. The anti-democratic ethnocracies on which these movements are constructed are henceforth only conduits for imperialist domination and nothing else.

Social movements are rarely multidimensional. The terrains on which they operate are almost always completely delimited by their original constitution. Unions, a feminist organization, and environmental organizations remain what they are. There is nothing disturbing in that, even if, without any ill will, one is right to pose questions about the underlying perspectives within which these movements operate. For example, is equality between men and women possible without moving beyond processes of capitalist reproduction? Is not the short-term financial logic of capitalism to eliminate the impact of environmental projects?

Beyond that, it remains the case that the specificity of the chosen terrain of action implicitly carries the possibility of strategic incoherence on the part of the actors in question. The nature of the action undertaken in these circumstances, whether progressive or not, remains subject to possible questioning. Numerous movements supporting democratic political claims have been, consequently, incapable of participating in the progressive transformations of their societies but have, rather, contributed to driving them into regression. I have in mind the movements of the supposed revolutions (Rose, Orange, etc.) in the countries of the former Soviet Union (Ukraine, Georgia, etc.). Not that the critiques that these movements addressed to the authorities against which they called for insurrection were without foundation. These critiques were perfectly justified. But these movements combined their (in appearance, at least) democratic demands with their support for global liberalism. They were, consequently, manipulated by the CIA and have not made any progress in the cause of democracy. These tragic experiences remind us that the causes of social progress and democracy cannot be separated. Unfortunately, we will have to conclude, then, that these movements, despite their democratic dress, were completely reactionary.

Democratic movements of this type are far from having exhausted their potential use. Most of the political regimes in contemporary Asia and Africa suffer from serious democratic deficits, to say the least. The United States, supported by its subaltern European allies, can, in these conditions, nourish the illusions that it is a matter of promoting democracy. A curious evolution becomes apparent here, one for which the Egyptian example provides an amusing illustration. The comprador bourgeoisies in Asia and Africa, which have rarely displayed democratic convictions, are suddenly converted into democratic liberals applauded by Washington for practicing "alternation" (in Egypt, they are in competition with the declining techno-bureaucrats and rising political Islam).[14] These liberals have taken the precaution of subscribing in advance to the dogmas of economic and social neoliberalism and of advertising their support for Washington's armed diplomacy.

TRUE AND FALSE CONFLICTS IN THE CONTEMPORARY WORLD

The fundamental conflict by which the entire modern era is defined is the conflict between labor (dominated, oppressed, and exploited) and capital (dominator and exploiter). In no way does this mean that every conflict occurring on the political and social scene can be reduced directly to this fundamental conflict or even that the historical actors in these conflicts assess their connection to it. Furthermore, the conflict between capital and labor functions in global imperialism through the contradiction between the dominated peripheries and dominant centers. This does not mean that the societies of the centers and peripheries are homogeneous blocs. On the contrary, the same fundamental contradiction runs through them, but in a different manner. The task of historical materialism, in my interpretation, is precisely to analyze the way in which all of these articulations function and, on that basis, elucidate the possible developments that they open, regardless of whether they be positive or negative, for the advance of socialism, humanism, and universalism.

Conflicts that, in appearance, occupy the forefront do not necessarily have the significance that their direct expression evokes. Here I will look at three dominant contemporary examples.

First, what is called the "clash of civilizations" is, in reality, a political strategy developed systematically by the collective imperialism of the triad and formulated in ideological terms by the United States. This strategy is all the more effective in its effects insofar as the social movements on the side of the system's victims adopt its themes and thereby contribute to making it a reality.

Second, the struggle for democracy against all forms of autocracy and oppression has never been separable, from either the struggles of workers and victims of exploitation or from the struggles of dominated peoples for their liberation. But there are social and political forces that proceed from this separation and maintain that it is possible and necessary to do so. I contend that, having done so, the movements concerned are manipulated by dominant capital and do not advance the cause of democracy itself. Whereas in the United States and Europe a large segment of public opinion may believe in the sincerity of the interventions of their countries in favor of democracy, it should be remembered that in Asia and Africa this so-called democratic rhetoric has no credibility.

Third, the conflict between the civilized and the terrorists, which we hear about constantly, is there only to hide the real conflict between imperialism and the peoples that it wants to dominate. The U.S. establishment has been preparing the manufacture of this new enemy for at least twenty years by developing a discourse on the possibility of private organizations equipping themselves with means of mass destruction and relying on the possible support of "rogue states" and, simultaneously, by contributing to the effective emergence of terrorist groups (support by the CIA for Islamic fundamentalist groups, the possible passive if not active complicity in the events of September 11th, which happened just in time, and the immediate promulgation of laws and measures ready for many years).

The intervention of the centers of the modern world system into the peripheries has always been, since 1492, in the service of consolidating imperialist domination, whatever be the proclaimed motives. The motives put forward today, whether exporting democracy or fighting against terrorism, are no better than those proclaimed yesterday (the "civilizing mission"). The terrible consequences of the interventions under way in the context of the Greater Middle East project demonstrate once more, as if that were necessary, that no intervention of the United States or NATO, even if disguised by a United Nations' resolution, whatever its motives (even so-called humanitarian ones) and in whatever region of the world it may occur (including Europe, for example in Yugoslavia), is defensible. The duty of European democratic forces is quite simply to demand the dissolution of NATO and the dismantling of U.S. bases as well as the immediate withdrawal from Afghanistan, Iraq, and occupied Palestine. I refer here to the proposals made in the Bamako Appeal (reproduced here in Appendix 2). However, note that the responsibility of the European democratic forces, as important as they may be, should not enable the democratic forces in the countries of the South, and particularly in the Arab countries, to forget their responsibilities.

THE PLUTOCRACY: NEW RULING CLASS OF OBSOLESCENT CAPITALISM

The process of accumulation is manifested in the growing concentration and centralization of capital. Competition, whose real but also completely imaginary virtues are praised by the system's ideology, still remains. But it is no more than competition among an increasingly smaller number of oligopolies. There is neither "perfect" competition nor "transparency," which has never existed. In fact, the more really existing capitalism develops, the further it is from such conditions. Now we have reached a level of centralization in the power of capital's domination such that the forms of existence and organization of the bourgeoisie known until now have been abolished.

The bourgeoisie was formed from stable bourgeois families. From one generation to another, the heirs continued a certain specialization in the activities of their companies. The bourgeoisie was constructed and constructed itself over a long period of time. This stability encouraged confidence in bourgeois values and their dissemination throughout the entire society. To a large extent, the bourgeoisie, the dominant class, was accepted as such. For the services it rendered, it appeared to deserve access to the privileges of luxury and wealth. It also appeared to be broadly national, sensitive to the interests of the nation, whatever the ambiguities and limits of this malleable and manipulated concept. The new ruling class of contemporary capitalism, emerging from the evolution of the last thirty years, has quite suddenly broken with this tradition. The Enron scandal and several others of the same kind have unquestionably contributed to revealing the nature of the transformation. Not that there has been no prior history of fraud, of course. What is much more serious, and new, is that the dominant logic necessarily gives rise to the search for the maximum level of opaqueness, deceit, even the systematic falsification of information. Some describe the transformation in question as "financialization," others as the development of active shareholders (even people's shareholders) completely reestablishing the rights of property. These laudatory descriptions, which in a certain way legitimize the change, fail to recognize, that the major aspect of the transformation concerns the degree of the concentration of capital and the centralization of power that is connected to it.

Doubtless, a large concentration of capital is not new. From the end of the nineteenth century, what Rudolf Hilferding, John Hobson, and Lenin described as a capitalism of monopolies has been a reality. Unquestionably, this concentration has always been, since then, more advanced in the United States than in other countries of central capitalism. The formation of the very large corporation, which later became a transnational corporation, began in the United States before the Second World War and spread triumphantly afterward, as Europe followed suit. Also it is unquestionable that the American ideology of the "self-made man" (the Rockefellers, Fords, and others) contrasts sharply with the family conservatism of Europe. This is also he case with the cult of true competition, even when it does not actually exist. This explains the early antitrust laws, beginning in 1890. But beyond these real differences in the political cultures, the same transformation in capitalism's new ruling class characterizes Europe as well as the United States.

The new ruling class can be counted on the fingers of just a few hands, hardly more. Moreover, a good proportion of this class is formed from newcomers who have asserted themselves more through the success of their financial operations—notably in the stock market—than through their contribution to the technological breakthroughs distinctive of our era. Their extremely rapid rise strongly contrasts with their predecessors, whose rise was spread out over numerous decades. The profusion of "start-ups" is also a new characteristic. The extreme instability leads to the failure of practically all of these ambitious newcomers, despite the celebratory rhetoric developed around them.

The centralization of power is even more marked than the concentration of capital, at the level of productive corporations as much as financial conglomerates. This centralization reinforces the interpenetration of economic and political power. Once again, this interpenetration is not new. After all, the class nature of power, even if it is democratic, means that the ruling political class is at the service of capital. Conversely, capitalist fortune has always invited certain men of power to share in the profits. But it seems that this interpenetration tends toward homogenization, which is new and is expressed in transformations of ideological discourse.

The traditional ideology of capitalism placed emphasis on the virtues of property in general, particularly small property, though in actual fact medium or medium-large property, which was considered to be a vehicle for technological and social progress because of its stability. In contrast, the new ideology heaps praise on the "winners" and scorns the "losers" without any other consideration. The dominant rhetoric deceptively puts forward the image of success in order to attribute failures to personal circumstances and, consequently, eliminate the responsibility of the social system. Is it necessary to point out that this ideology, which calls to mind a sort of social Darwinism is close to that which regulates relations among members of a criminal organization? The winner here is almost always right, even when the means used, though not statutory criminal offenses, border on the illegal and, in any case, ignore common moral values.

The concrete expression of the judgment made here is the complicity between the business world and institutions responsible for auditing and rating, and the at least tacit complicity of public authorities. The rhetoric about transparency is, in light of this reality, only a second-rate propagandistic discourse.

The particular nature of the mode of financing for firms in the United States, i.e., the recourse to the financial market (issuing of stocks and bonds) instead of the support of banks and the state (through specialized public institutions), it is said, is the origin of this situation. That is partially true. Yet it is also true that the German and Japanese models, which favor financial integration between banks and companies, or the French model, based on interventions by state financial institutions, have not protected the European systems from the same kinds of abuses.

The fundamental reason for the developments in question lies in the high level of the centralization of capital. There is no possible comparison with what it was three decades ago. The complicity between economic power and political power, which merge to become just simply power, takes us back to what Marx and Fernand Braudel said about capitalism: it is not reducible to the market (as the dominant discourse repeats *ad nauseam*) but, on the contrary, is to be identified with powers above the market (the oligopolies and the state). That this convergence today, in the "new capitalism," is as strong as it was at the beginning of capitalism (in the Republic of Venice, administered as a limited–liability company of the wealthiest merchants, or in the Colbertist and Elizabethan era of the absolute monarchies), after having been strongly limited in the nineteenth and twentieth centuries, only testifies to the fact that the system has indeed become obsolete and has entered into its senescent phase.

Contemporary capitalism has become, through the force of its own logic of accumulation, a crony capitalism (*capitalisme de connivence*). This term can no longer be reserved just for the underdeveloped and corrupt forms of Southeast Asia and Latin America, which the "true economists" (i.e., the sincere and convinced believers in the virtues of liberalism) denounced only yesterday. From now on, it also applies to capitalism in the United States and contemporary Europe. The current behavior of this ruling class is similar to that of the mafia, even though this description might appear insulting and extreme.

The system does not know how to react to this situation, quite simply because it is not able to call into question the centralization of capital. Oddly, the measures taken recall the antitrust laws at the end of the nineteenth century (the Sherman Act), the limited effectiveness of which is well known. In complete agreement with the tradition of the United States, the society responds by an intensified recourse to moralism and government by the judiciary. In the Enron affair, Eliot Spitzer, then New York State attorney general, garnered much publicity by exhibiting, in a well-prepared media show, millionaires in handcuffs, never seen before in the United States. The 2002 Sarbanes-Oxley Act will legitimize greater intervention by judges in the activities of companies. I bet such actions will end up becoming part of the game of complicity that they are meant to eradicate.

Europe was equipped to react differently. Its political culture is characterized by suspicion of moralism and government by the judiciary. Instead, preference is given to legislative regulation. Further, financing is less subject to the uncertainties of the financial market. As a result, Europe was not condemned by the supposedly implacable demand of the economy to conform to the model characterized by the apparent dictatorship of the financial market (the stock exchange). The latter is manipulated by a small oligarchy. However, Europe did fall into line with the United States against its actual interests, since the open financial market in question quite simply makes it possible for pension funds from the United States to seize the best segments of the European economies (in particular, the French economy, where 50 percent of the capital quoted on the stock exchange is controlled by the United States) and skim off the profits. The reason for this apparently absurd behavior is the desire of large capital never to clash with "big brother," who is the ultimate guarantor of the capitalist order—"Better Hitler than the Popular Front."

In the longer term, a new formation of the European Left, in line with its political culture, is obviously capable of challenging this situation. But that could probably not be done without calling capitalism into question, at least in some of its essential aspects. The democratic advances through which this reconstruction of the Left could take place, in turn, would call into question the current models of centralized oligarchic authority. But the European Left is, unfortunately, not following that path.

The political system of contemporary capitalism is, henceforth, a plutocratic system. The latter adapts itself to the continued practice of representative democracy, which has become "low-intensity democracy": you are free to vote for whomever you want, though that is of no importance, since it is the market and not Parliament that decides everything. Elsewhere, it adapts itself to autocratic forms of power or electoral farces.

CHAPTER THREE

WHAT TO DO?

POLITICAL CULTURES OF CONFLICT AND POLITICAL CULTURES OF CONSENSUS

Our political culture[15] is based on the recognition of conflict—not only as an expression of reality, but also as bearer of positive, liberating advances. This political culture has been crystallized from the history of modern Europe, punctuated by a succession of great moments: the Enlightenment, the French Revolution, the emergence of the socialist and Marxist movement, the Russian Revolution. "Right" and "Left" are strongly defined by their stand in regard to these great moments. If one is for the Enlightenment (Locke and the French eighteenth century), one is on the Left. If one is anti-Enlightenment (from Edmund Burke, Louis Gabriel Ambroise de Bonald, Joseph de Maistre and Johann Gottfried von Herder at the beginning to the exalters of anti-communism of which Isaac Berlin is the standard bearer, to the neocons of the United States and the postmodernists), one is on the Right. If one is for the French Revolution, one is on the Left. If against it (up to Furet), one is on the Right. Again, if one is for the workers' movement and socialism (including Marxism) or against them (with the conservative Right, then the fascists and finally the eulogizers of the liberal consensus today), then one is Left or Right, respectively. The Russian Revolution imposes the same distinction.

In moments of intense struggle, as in revolutions (the French Revolution, 1848, the Paris Commune, the Russian Revolution), the distinction is sharp and the oppositions extreme.

A great number of intellectuals rally to the side of the people in struggle. In periods of restoration, always partial but nevertheless real, which come between the revolutions, the sharpness of the distinction loses its edge. Helplessness grabs hold of the Left, intellectuals become "traitors"[16] and place themselves at the service of the authorities, and reformists drift away from radicalism toward insignificant cosmetic proposals. Opinions are won over to—or submit to—a political culture of "consensus." This consensus, of course, protects the social interests of dominant capital and, consequently, is on the Right. The consensus that brings Democrats and Republicans together in the United States is the recognition of the permanently sacred character of property, the consensus characterized by rallying to social-liberalism, the very real current political projects of forming large coalitions of the center in Italy, Germany, and elsewhere—all of these show that we are indubitably in a period of decline of this type.

The view that one has about social movements cannot avoid dealing with the characteristics of the moment: is it a moment of advance—including a revolutionary one—or a moment of withdrawal?

The political culture of conflict proceeds from the recognition that society is traversed by fundamental social contradictions, by the class struggle. But at the same time, and certainly not by chance, ideological struggle is no less fundamental. The Left acts in favor of emancipation, liberation from various types of alienation (particularly, the economic alienation of capitalism), in the hope of eradicating oppression and the exploitation of labor. Undoubtedly, these positions only come together gradually—the feminist cause was ignored for a long time, alleviating the extreme forms of exploitation of workers is undertaken at the same time creative utopian views are proposed to eradicate it, etc. Enlightenment philosophy defined the modernity that it inaugurated on the basis of emancipating Reason. By proclaiming that human beings make—have to make—their history, individually and collectively, the Enlightenment broke with the traditional thinking dominant in the Christian Europe of the *Ancien Régime*, and elsewhere in the history of humanity, which transferred this responsibility exclusively to God, to nature, or to ancestors. The individual was affirmed as the subject of history. This is the "creative utopia" of the communism of Marx and others. Liberation theology offers irrefutable proof that this is compatible with belief in God by separating such belief from support for the sacredness of the unjust social order, which the conservative interpretation of religion merges together. The development of this project, beginning with the Enlightenment, gradually gives rise to the awareness that the emancipation in question requires transformation of the social order through class conflict.

Unquestionably, the meaning and scope of the concept of emancipation are going to be expanded through its development in directions that are barely imaginable, or not possible at all, at the beginning. I have already given the example of feminism. The ecological dimension of the challenge (whose distant roots could be pointed out) emerges later. It is known today that capitalism is not viable, ultimately, because of the ecological destruction that the logic of its development makes inevitable. It is also known today that just preserving the forms of consumption that benefit a minority of some twenty percent of humanity requires that the aspirations of the others to a better life must be ruthlessly crushed. Although all the quantitative data concerning this challenge are undoubtedly known and recognized, nothing changes because the beneficiaries of the system cannot possible envisage the sacrifices ("intellectual suicide") that the emancipation of everyone imposes on them.

Rejection of the Enlightenment, emancipation, and socialism is the foundation for the thinking of the Right. Even when it belatedly dons the clothes of "liberalism" (in the political sense of the term: acceptance of representative democracy, universal suffrage, etc.), it never truly abandons this rejection.

The "hard" Right bluntly asserts its anti-Enlightenment position. Burke, Herder, de Bonald, and de Maistre unreservedly condemn what they say is the excessive ambition of emancipatory Reason. They then express their commitment to a political culture that they claim is one of consensus, defined as the voluntary submission of everyone (rich and poor, powerful and weak) to membership in the same community, Christian or national (for Herder it was the German nation, substituting *gemeinschaft* for *gesellschaft*).[17] That we see this consensus as never having had any real foundation is not the question. The ideology of the Right asserts it can, in certain circumstances, use it effectively.

Political liberalism has succeeded to various degrees in giving complete effectiveness to the illusion of a possible consensus beyond the class struggle and the ideological conflict by which the Right and Left are defined. Certainly, the class struggle never ceases to have an impact, but it is kept in check by the adherence to representative democracy, which is based on constitutional principles that invoke respect for property, while ideological conflicts—for or against the Enlightenment, for or against socialism—are reduced to the status of ordinary debates on ideas.

The fact remains that, although political liberalism is devoted to substituting a political culture of consensus for one of conflict, its association with nationalism is the means for success in doing so. The objective reality of the global and unequal expansion of capitalism reasserts itself here. This reality is expressed in the imperialist form of expansion (the contrast between dominant centers and dominated peripheries), which makes it possible for significant segments of the working classes to be won over to social-colonialism. It is also expressed in the constant clash of the imperialist centers in competition, which makes the success of nationalist ideologies easier. The moderate Right and the "pink" Left that joins it find themselves in competition with the hard Right on the latter's own terrain.

Moments characterized by the domination of the culture of conflict or by that of consensus follow one another in an ebb and flow with the rise and fall of the great events identified above. The discourse of consensus is certainly on the offensive at the current time. This is expressed in what appears to be the "Americanization" of political life in Europe. This term is all the more appropriate since the political culture of the United States is based on the assertion of consensus and subsequently is deployed almost constantly within this context through the renewal of its effective forms of expression. I refer here to the comparative analysis that I have offered elsewhere[18] of this contrast between the political cultures of the United States and Europe. This contrast implies a significant political divergence whose solution will decide the fate of the European project. To either remain within the limits of the European wing of the Atlanticist project under the hegemony of the United States or to assert itself by renewing a Left perspective ("The European project will be Left or it will not be," I have written in this connection) is the question which Europe faces today.

The political culture of conflict came out of Europe. Capitalist globalization and its expansion, are at the origin of the globalization of the conflict between the peoples of the peripheries and dominant capitalist imperialism. In some situations, this conflict merges with the conflict between the revolutionary perspective of communism and submission to the unequal order of imperialism. The Third International was the vehicle for these radicalizations, embodied in the Chinese, Vietnamese, and Cuban revolutions. Radical national liberation movements (in the past, those associated with the wars of liberation in Algeria and the Portuguese colonies, the national populism of Nasserism and, more generally, the spirit of Bandung; in the present, those emerging among Latin American peoples) express the same sort of radicalization. The conflict is also expressed through a deep cleave between the Left and the Right, both inside the societies concerned and in world opinion: the Left parades behind pictures of Ho Chi Minh and Che Guevara, defends Nasserist Egypt when it is attacked, while the Right vows an implacable hatred for the Bandung leaders and vilifies Castro.

But here also, on the periphery, moments of withdrawal, such as ours, show a loss of any sense of the distinction between the Left and the Right. Peoples who resist imperialist aggression are disoriented and agree to line up behind questionable leaders who wave the flag of religious or ethnic identity. Bin Laden, the ex-

CIA man who is named by the corporate media as enemy number one, consequently benefits from the sympathy of many of the victims of imperialist aggression. The heir of the slave system of the Buddhist lamas, the Dalai Lama (known as a "humanist"), the Latvian Nazis (who erected a monument in praise of the SS without any voice of protest being heard in Europe), and the fanatics of the so-called Christian sects in the United States also benefit from such sympathy. It is no longer a question of a political culture of conflict, but simply a matter of the manipulation of violence to the benefit of the interests that dominate the system. The clash of barbarisms, as Gilbert Achcar quite rightly analyzes it, has taken the place of the true clash of civilizations of our time—the clash between the socialist perspective and capitalist reality.

THE WORLD WE WANT: TWO THEORIES OF SOCIETY, TWO VISIONS OF THE FUTURE

It is helpful to emphasize the opposition between the "liberal" (as the term is used in the United States) theory of the individual and society and the one proposed in the tradition of the Enlightenment, the French Revolution, and Marxism. I am using the singular for the latter despite the multiplicity of interpretations involved.

Competition or Solidarity?

In a particular reading that extrapolates Darwin to social phenomena, after having, moreover, misinterpreted Darwin's understanding of evolution, liberal philosophy establishes competition as the principal driving force of progress. As a counterpoint, we will put forward, as Peter Kropotkin maintained, that solidarity has created far more constructive functions in history, regardless of whether this be the organization of an effective system for the management of work or solidarity in the class struggle (the solidarity of workers is the basis for their conquests), or whether this solidarity has been built between equals or within a hierarchical framework.

Individual or Citizen?

Liberal doctrine defines society as a collection of individuals, whether they are imagined to be equal in principle because of their potential capabilities or their rights (meaning that individuals are by right equal before God and should be equal before the law) or imagined to be essentially unequal. In the latter case, inequality legitimizes the positions of the winners and losers produced by competition. As a counterpoint, I will emphasize the organization by which any society is defined, which is never a sum of individuals. This structure can be hierarchical (it has always been so in history and still is), be it in the area of economic production or organization of authority (governing and governed), or democratic. It is possible to imagine another structure, one that eliminates inequalities. This would not be reduced to the juxtaposition of individuals declared to be equal, because achieving the conditions for their equality requires adequate forms of organization. The individual, whose reality is recognized, as is the assertion of a desired personality, is thus a citizen, in the sense of being an active member of an organized political society.

Communitarian Withdrawal or Full Development of Political Parties?

The individuals defined by liberalism cannot endure the isolation in which the free play of competition imprisons them. The antidote, then, is to search for compensatory solidarities. Communitarianism (ethnic or para-ethnic, neighborhoods or professions, most often religious and sectarian) is the expression of that antidote. The lives of the persons concerned are governed by a schizophrenia expressed in the juxtaposition between moments of unlimited individualism (in competition at work, for example) and "communions" in rapture (every member of the sect paying obeisance to their guru). In contrast, citizenship functions in another way to give meaning to the aspirations of the individual. Its normal way of functioning calls for the formation of political parties, that is, organizations that rally individuals around a project for a specific society, whether it be defined through a specific class consciousness (such as in workers' or socialist parties) or through a particular political viewpoint (such as proposed by national parties for secular democracy, advanced democracy, or even the fascist management of power). Recognition of conflicts of interest as well as the diversity of ideas is essential to the functioning of citizenship.

Consensus or Inventive Democracy?

Liberal democracy is not authentically pluralist because it avoids conflict and seeks consensus. The latter is the only means to prevent competition between individuals, the fundamental principle around which liberal society is built, from degenerating into chaotic and criminal anarchy. Recognition that there is no alternative to the existing world as it is, i.e., capitalism, is expressed through consensus. Conflicts of interest are thus only conflicts of particular and partial interests that can and must be reconciled. The good technocrat is able to offer solutions, after having heard the lobbyists advance their arguments. Radical political parties hinder more than contribute to the achievement of consensus. Consensus assumes that all subversions can be diluted and ultimately absorbed. The ideal is thus "bipartisanship" as found in the United States, in which the two parties are joined together on the main principles even if they address supporters (above all not social classes!) with different tastes. Consensus is imposed on everyone. The Constitution is sacred and it is absolutely unimaginable that it is possible to replace it with another one (which is not the case in Europe!) and private property provides the inviolable foundation for the permanence of this mode of social organization (no horizon beyond capitalism is imaginable). In contrast, the very definition of democracy is the right to innovation, invention, and imagination. Since nothing in the current social organization is sacred, democracy becomes subversive by nature. Subversion is the driving force of social transformation. Radical democrats do not like consensus, and when it appears to be operating in their society—in situations of war, for example—they are suspicious of its destructive effects on the critical spirit.

Socialization through the Market or Socialization through Democracy?

Liberalism practices "old-style" politics; that is, the conventional politics of representative democracy associated with the management of the economy through private property and the market. The economic and the political are separate. The economic is depoliticized. The democracy at work in these conditions, which functions by consensus, is flat and even empty. It cannot go against what the market (today that means capitalism dominated by the oligopolies) requires. Socialization occurs exclusively through the market. This principle is completely consistent with the concept of society as a collection of individuals. The principles and language of the market are extrapolated to all kinds of human activities. There is a political market, a market of ideas, market of the arts, marriage market, etc. In contrast, radical democracy conceives the objective to be socialization through democracy. This implies that politics are the subject of continual inventiveness, not reduced to the implementation of principles that are defined once and for all. Consequently, it politicizes the principles for managing economic affairs. If it sees a possible association between the two forms of socialization, through democracy and through the market, it intends to give the last word to democracy. Regulation of the market, and not its maximum freedom, is the means by which radical democracy can lay down this vision for continual democratic inventiveness.

HOW TO DO POLITICS

The way of doing politics typical of the critical Left forces of the last century (in particular, the Second, Third, and Fourth Internationals) has been rejected once and for all by new generations of militants and the movements they lead. This tradition is reproached, and rightly so, for the undemocratic practices on which it was based: rejection of diversity; the claim of some to hold the "correct line" deduced from a "scientific" analysis that is asserted to be irreproachable; the marked centralization of organization and decision-making authorities (in parties, unions and associated movements); bureaucratic and doctrinaire excesses that were fatal in these conditions, etc. The concept of the vanguard is, consequently, rejected as eminently dangerous.

This critique must be taken seriously and accepted in its essential points. In this sense, the principles of diversity and democratic management, which lie behind the coming together of the movements in the World Social Forum, must be completely respected without concession.

The diversity in question is multidimensional and involves both theory and practice. The diversity of explicit or implicit analyses is found not only across the range of resistance and struggle in the present time but often traverses some of the movements themselves. The extreme positions held by different groups or individuals concerning the relation between theory and practice are a clear illustration of the extent of this diversity. At one pole of the spectrum are those who, taking a well-known (and probably simplified) Leninist thesis, assert that theory has to be brought into the movement from the outside. Others substitute, or combine, the imagination of creative utopia with theory. At the other pole of the spectrum are those who assert that the future can only be the natural and spontaneous product of the movement.

To accept diversity certainly demands tolerance of a range of viewpoints. Doing that means holding a viewpoint that accepts that the future is the product both of the movement and preliminary conceptions formulated about it. I will define the objective (which I continue to call socialism/communism) as the simultaneous product of theory and practice, the product of their gradual convergence. The aim is not to entail, *a priori*, any prerequisite theory decreed as "Right" or any view defined prior to the end of the development in question. Reactionary forces exert systematic efforts to legitimize conflicts of cultures that are supposedly based on invariants transmitted by historical heritage, particularly religious ones. The internationalism of peoples must fight these cultural interpretations and place at the forefront the modern era's true conflict of cultures: between the values of socialism and the culture of capitalism.

I will go even further and propose the idea that diversity also concerns visions of the future as well as their ethical and cultural bases. Marxism, radical reformism, liberation theology, anarchism, feminism, and radical environmentalism in all of their varieties, have a necessary place in the construction of convergence in diversity.

Organizing convergence while respecting diversity does not exclude confrontation between different viewpoints but rather implies it, so long as the purpose of this confrontation is not to excommunicate the unbelievers.

Having arrived at this point, I will formulate here my own proposals. The movement by itself, in its spontaneity, cannot produce any desirable future. It is not possible for it to move out of chaos. This is all the more true if the movement declares itself to be apolitical. One part of the movement—for perfectly respectable ethical motives and because the observation that power corrupts refers to real historical experiences—refuses to give itself the objective of attaining power. The enthusiastic support that Subcommandante Marcos and the Zapatista movement have received reflects, to a great extent, to this standpoint. Unquestionably, this position can be justified in particular times and places. But certainly a general rule, valid for the future (and even already the present) cannot be drawn from this consideration. More generally, the apolitical option (or at least a definition of the political that is close to it), which Michael Hardt and Antonio Negri have formulated (in connection with their post-imperialist thesis and not by chance), appears to me to be at best naïve and at worst a sign of their rallying to North American reactionary political culture (and its concept of apolitical civil society).

It is necessary today to practice politics in such a way as to take up the challenges of the current capitalist/imperialist systems and be capable of producing a possible, positive alternative consists in managing diversity as it was done in the First International—and not as it was done in the subsequent Internationals. Further, I am struck by the similarity between the debates in the First International and those in the World Social Forum.

Indeed, the refusal of politics exhibited by numerous movements proceeds from their fear that in political parties the organizational logic ends up prevailing over the logic of struggle. This observation is certainly not unfounded. Nonetheless, the fact remains that the logic of organization prevails above all in small organizations or movements that pretend to be "non-organized." The choice is not between politics or no politics, but the logic of organization or the logic of struggle.

CONSTRUCTING CONVERGENCE IN DIVERSITY

Constructing the convergence of all the movements and social and political forces through which the victims of global capitalism express themselves certainly demands respect for diversity in at least five dimensions:

1. The degree of radicalism in the critique of capitalism. Those who are close to the ardent supporters of neoliberalism, having accepted its essential requirements, propose cosmetic reforms intended to save capitalism from the excesses of neoliberalism (as George Soros would have it). The World Bank's discourse (including that of Joseph Stiglitz) and the programs that are proposed to reduce poverty (without calling into question the neoliberal system that causes it) participate in this strategy, whose real objective is to weaken popular movements, not strengthen them. There are moderate reformists who, in the current conjuncture, take up the defense of threatened rights (social security, education and health, etc.) and radical reformists whose proposals are open to social processes that lead beyond capitalism and are thus close to the positions of those who adopt a socialist perspective.

2. The degree of radicalism in the critique of capitalist globalization. For some, there is no alternative to globalization, but it is still potentially positive: it offers opportunities that must be seized. Others insist on the imperialist dimension of really existing capitalist globalization, particularly its neoliberal form, as well as the reality of the hegemony of the United States.

3. The degree of radicalism in the conception of democracy that is advanced. Openly anti-democratic standpoints exist in

the South and the former East among the new classes and the comprador powers that support the neoliberal project. Such standpoints exist, as well, in the United States (the so-called Christian and fundamentalist Right rallies nearly half of the Republican electorate) and in traditionally democratic Europe (Joerg Haider-type neo-populisms, Silvio Berlusconi and others). In the center exists the great majority who are satisfied with the practices of minimalist democracy, from electoral buffooneries (in the United States and throughout the Third World) to "low-intensity democracy" based on a supposedly depoliticized consensus (the vote, whether it favors the parliamentary Right or Left, is thus devoid of any meaning since the governments that result accept the powerlessness in which the rules of the market confine them). The Left is defined by the struggle it leads to give democracy the emancipatory meaning it should have, encompassing straightaway all the dimensions of the challenge, with the intent of affirming the rights of the human being and citizen, individual and collective social rights, and the right to control the economic system. By radicalizing these demands, they become part of movements that aim at going beyond capitalism.

4. The degree of radicalism concerning relations between men and women. There are affirmed anti-feminist ideologies (generally claiming to adhere to religious fundamentalisms in the United States, the Islamic, Hindu, and Confucian worlds, etc.) as well as *de facto* male chauvinist behaviors. Some political currents are disposed to accept feminist demands on the condition that they do not call into question the fundamental capitalist order. Radical feminism, like radical democracy, is part of an emancipatory process that necessarily opens into perspectives that point beyond capitalism.

5. The degree of radicalism in the environmental critique of the dominant global system. The position taken by the United States, sacrificing the future of the planet for the immediate profits of transnational corporations and to maintain the (wasteful) American way of life cannot be ignored. Naïve environmentalists refuse to understand the extent of this destructive dimension of

capitalism, inseparable from the short-term horizon of financial calculation that defines the rationality of this mode of production. Consistent environmentalists join socialists in their uncompromising critique of capitalist rationality.

In the space defined by these five dimensions of the challenge, some regions are practically empty because the combination of the criteria taken into consideration is too contradictory for them to coexist. Others are, on the contrary, sites for the concentration of dominant Right forces, while many social and political movements that form the potential of the Left alternative are scattered across the space under consideration.

To support neoliberal theses and the associated view of dominant globalization means today to be on the Right, even when one dons a Left electoral hat (a frequent case in Europe) or supports a discourse (but only a discourse) with anti-imperialist and nationalist pretensions (a possible situation in the South). The hegemonic Right is at best moderately reformist, based on a democratic "consensus" in the sense that the term has acquired in current discourse. This Right, which is in the majority in Europe, includes, particularly in the United States, undemocratic ideological and social movements that are violently anti-feminist and racist. The Republican establishment has integrated a so-called moral front into the alliance in power. On the peripheries of the South and former Eastern bloc, the comprador Right, which holds most of the current governments, finds its social base in the "racketeer" circles fostered by neoliberal globalization. This term racketeer, currently used in the Third World and in the former Soviet countries, expresses quite well the nature and the ultimate fragility of this undemocratic, artificial, and not very enterprising bourgeoisie.

The Left that should be built is radically anti-neoliberal, at least anti-hegemonist, if not anti-imperialist, and progressively democratic. But all the forces and movements engaged in the contemporary struggles against the authorities of the dominant Right do not necessarily line up behind these positions. There is, occasionally in the capitalist centers, a radical Left that is not very sensitive to the imperialist dimension of the system. Currently, anti-imperialist consciousness is certainly, throughout the North, very weak: the excesses of the national liberation movements around which "Third Worldist" Western youth had been mobilized contributed to their later disappointments. On the peripheries, there is nostalgia for Soviet-style systems and undemocratic populisms that nevertheless were critical of neoliberalism and imperialism. Other segments of the political and ideological forces on the peripheries, which certainly have more future potential, aspire to defend legitimate national interests. Some of the governments in the regions concerned appear to have rallied to globalization and accepted the hegemony of the United States only because they have been constrained to do so, reckoning that the balance of power does not allow them to refuse. At the current time, these forces navigate between the illusion of a relatively undemocratic nationalism of the Right, therefore agreeing to be part of a global neoliberalism with which they believe they can negotiate, and possibly rallying to an anti-imperialist democratic popular front. It is on this condition alone that these forces can acquire real power and rejoin the camp of the world Left that is being built. Otherwise they are condemned to remain indecisive, perhaps even to be attracted by diversions such as those represented by chauvinistic ethnic movements or pseudo-religious fundamentalisms (political Islam and Hinduism, for example). Anti-democratic movements, which *de facto* agree to submit their peoples to the requirements of capitalist globalization, despite their anti-Western, culturalist verbiage, in reality are part of the alliance of the world Right.

Constructing the alternative Left demands that strategies and tactics be developed in various places that call for gathering around the center-Left all political forces, all ideological currents, and all social movements engaged in struggle against neoliberalism and imperialism or even in favor of democratic advances, progress in the liberation of women and progress in respecting the requirements for a correct ecological management of the planet. It is possible to attract to the center-Left many movements that are fragmented and distributed across social space, thus illustrating our intention. There is no reason to think that reformists, defenders of democracy, the rights of women, peoples, and the environment, as well as pacifists, will remain unable to learn from the failure of the moderate options that still characterize most of their positions today. All will not be able to do so and this should be acknowledged and accepted. There will remain reformists, who will be satisfied with cosmetic changes without necessarily seeing that they are being used by the dominant Right. There will remain revolutionaries who will indefinitely accept being enclosed in doctrinaire ghettoes in order to evade the question of knowing how they might be able to help humanity progress in the direction of a revolutionary social project. It is also possible to push currents, perhaps even organizations, of anti-imperialist segments of public opinion in the countries of the South toward more coherent positions likely to gain them wide popular support. There will, nevertheless, always remain sections of these potential forces attracted by the comprador camp, just as there will be popular movements that will continue their deviation to the path of culturalism.

The hegemonic Right is much less solid than it appears. It is traversed by contradictions that are bound to be intensified in step with the apparent successes of its project. The bloc that forms this Right is bound to crack. The South, which the Right's project has nothing to offer, is formed of a series of "weak links" (China, India, Brazil, South Africa, and others). The North is bound to see the democratic, humanist and socialist tradition, deeply rooted in the history of Europe, established as a growing obstacle to uniting behind the appalling prospect of the United States' hegemony. Capitalism is certainly not an unsurpassable horizon as most ideologues and leaders of progressive popular movements still think today. In the immediate future, struggles undertaken against neoliberalism (an extremely reactionary form of capitalism) and the arrogance of American hegemony (spearhead of the new imperialism) will be driven to become more radical as advances are made in these directions.

The world will remain populated with those I will describe as "navigating politicians." I mean by this active and knowing men and women who remain prisoners of a fundamentally opportunist concept of politics, namely, that the latter is the art of benefiting from the balance of power, such as it is, while the radical and revolutionary define politics as being the art of transforming the balance of power. The navigating politicians are nevertheless sensitive to the opinions of segments of society on which their success depends (whether in a regime of electoral democracy or not). Most of them would join the camp of the Left, if, reconstructed, it brings about a reversal in the balance of power. They will not always do it because of vulgar opportunism and careerism, but because they rediscover on the Left all the values to which they are attached. Reformists, anti-imperialists, are, in part at least, motivated by our values.

The construction of convergence can be formulated in political terms in quite different ways, but still in ways that are complementary to one another. For instance: "For a united front in favor of social and international justice." Here we emphasize that the two qualifiers are inseparable, that social justice in the centers must be accompanied by a decidedly anti-imperialist consciousness, that anti-imperialism on the peripheries has no future if it is not borne by the working classes that need social justice and democracy. "The democratic state in the long transition beyond barbaric capitalism is a state that imposes citizen and social regulation." Or "Socialization by honest citizen and social democracy precludes socialization by the market." Or "There is no possible response to social needs without democracy and no democracy without responding to social needs."

These slogans draw their lessons from recent history. In the South, governments that have agreed to incorporate their desire for democratization within the limits imposed by neoliberalism contribute to discrediting democracy, leading either to a return to authoritarian populism or violent dictatorship in the service of imperialism. In the North, the Right-Left consensus (electoral majority) around economic liberalism substitutes the American form of "low-intensity democracy" for the citizen and social democracy of the historic Left, perpetuates conditions that fragment resistance and dashes the hope for a maturing of anti-imperialist consciousness.

OPENING THE DEBATE ON THE LONG TRANSITION TO SOCIALISM

Having recognized Lenin's error in his assessment of the real challenges and maturity of the revolutionary conditions, we must go beyond the critique and self-critique of the history of twentieth-century communism to open debate, overtly and inventively, on positive alternative strategies for the twentieth-first century. I will not return in detail to what I have proposed elsewhere, but will summarize the main points here:

1. We must envisage strategies that meet the challenge of the prospect for a long transition from world capitalism to world socialism.

2. Over the course of this long transition, the social, economic, and political systems produced by social struggles will combine, in reality, elements of the reproduction of capitalist society and, contradictorily, elements that are beginning and developing socialist social relations. These are two conflictual logics in permanent combination and contradiction.

3. Progress in this direction is necessary and possible in every region of the world capitalist system, in the imperialist centers as much as in its peripheries. Of course, interim strategies for these developments must, inevitably, be concrete and specific, notably concerning the center/periphery contrast.

4. Social, ideological, and political forces through which popular interests are expressed, even if confusedly, are already working in these directions. The so-called alternative globalization movements are material proof of that. It remains true that these movements convey different alternatives, some progressive (tending in the direction indicated above), others illusory or even outright reactionary (para-fascist responses to the challenges). Politicizing the debate, in the good and true sense of the term, is the condition for constructing what I have called the convergence in diversity of progressive forces.

5. The victims of the development of liberal capitalism include the majority in every region of the world. Socialism must be capable of mobilizing this new historical opportunity. But it will only be able to do so if it knows how to take into account transformations produced by technological revolutions, which have changed social structures completely and permanently. Communism must no longer be the flag of the industrial working class alone. It can become the future rallying point for a large majority of workers, despite the diversity in their status. Reconstructing the unity of workers, of those who benefit from stability in the system and those who are excluded from it, is today a major challenge for a communist renewal. In the peripheries, this reconstruction also implies the organization of vast movements capable of imposing the right of equal access to the land for all peasants. This renewal is all the more imperative since it is often forgotten that the peasantry still includes half of humanity and capitalism in all its forms is incapable of resolving this major problem.

An effective action strategy for the desired prospect must be capable of producing advances in three directions simultaneously: social progress, democratization, and construction of a multi-polar world system. The political democracy that is proposed to go along with the liberal capitalist economic option is bound to lead to a dramatic loss of all credibility for democracy. Conversely, social progress provided from above as a substitute for the invention of solutions through the development of the democratic power of the working classes is no longer acceptable. There will be no socialism without democracy, but equally there will be no democratic advances without social progress. Lastly, given the reality of diverse nations (and particularly the political cultures that form them) and the inequality produced by the history of the development of world capitalism, the opening of possibilities for social and democratic advances requires the construction of a multi-polar world system. The first condition of this is obviously the defeat of Washington's project for military control of the planet.

MEDIUM-TERM OBJECTIVES

For Europe, the challenge is structured around the central question of European institutions. The latter were designed for the systematic consolidation of Europe into economic liberalism and political Atlanticism. The European Commission is, in this sense, the perfect guarantee of the continuation of the power of European reaction. The calls for "another Europe," a "social Europe" will be a matter of pure incantation so long as this institutional construction is not called into question from top to bottom.

This construction of Europe has eliminated the sovereign powers of states, a foundation without which the exercise of democracy, for lack of any basis in reality, turns into farce. It has failed to substitute for those powers the formation of a federal (or confederal) power for which, moreover, the conditions of existence have not come together. This was obviously done to reduce really existing Europe to being only the European wing of the American political project (Atlanticism and the decisive role of NATO, led by Washington, in the actual foreign policy of Europe). Insofar as the action of the dominant forces of the collective imperialism of the triad is part of liberal globalization, European construction proceeds as the latter's instrument.

What in Europe is called the "plural Left," united in principle behind "alternation" within the limits imposed by liberal and Atlanticist European construction (and which, consequently, is not an alternative), is certainly not the means by which the peoples of this continent could envisage their exit from the tunnel. The reconstruction of "another Left" is the condition without which it is difficult to imagine the prospect of European peoples exercising power. All the same, in these conditions, are the contradictions between Europe and the United States bound to appear with increasing intensity? Some attribute to that the probability (whether they desire it or deplore it) of conflict between the economic interests of the dominant firms in the two geographic areas. I am not convinced by this argument. On the contrary, I believe that the contrast that separates the political culture of Europe from that of the United States presages a political conflict whose first manifestations are already visible. The reaffirmation of the political cultures of Europe, threatened by the Americanization of the continent, has, in my opinion, great potential for a renaissance of a Left equal to the challenge, that is, one that is anti-liberal and anti-Atlanticist. Liberalism is the enemy of democracy and its implementation results in the erosion of democratic traditions, wherever they exist. Important fractions of the Right in the countries concerned unhesitatingly line up behind the exercise of anti-democratic authority. But other political forces, notably those represented by social democratic parties, remain attached to the defense of the democracy that they believe is possible to reconcile with their alignment with liberalism. The struggle against liberalism cannot ignore this real contradiction.

The peoples of the three continents (Asia, Africa, Latin America) are confronted today with a system that is, in many respects, analogous to the one in place at the end of the Second World War: a colonial system that does not recognize their sovereign rights, imposes on them the economic system that is convenient for the oligopolies of the imperialist center, even the appropriate political systems. The expansion of the neoliberal system over the last few decades is no less than the construction of apartheid on a world scale.

Bandung had been the response to the same challenge by the states, nations, and peoples of Asia and Africa in 1955. These were states formed in the aftermath of the victory of revolutions conducted under the banners of socialism or powerful national liberation movements and which consequently benefited from an established legitimacy. Moreover, the coalitions that formed the revolutionary blocs and the national liberation movements, beyond their certain diversity, always included at least significant segments of those forces aspiring to be the ruling capitalist bourgeoisie in the new society, even though they would not have been able, at the time, to carry out management of the state on their own. This bourgeois dimension of Bandung, which was manifested in the vision of development implemented at the time, rehabilitated the national bourgeoisie, whose historical role had been considered definitively closed in the earlier stage of the immediate postwar world. The turbulent relations between the ambitions of this bourgeoisie, on the one hand, and the aspirations of the working classes, on the other, shaped the history of the Bandung decades.

The new imperialist order will be called into question. But who will question it? And what will result from this? Such are the challenges confronting the states and peoples on the peripheries today.

Undoubtedly, the current picture of the dominant reality does not leave much room for hope of an immediate questioning of this order. The failed ruling classes in the countries of the South have largely accepted their role of subaltern compradors. The helpless peoples, engaged in a struggle for daily survival, appear often to accept their lot or even worse, to nourish new illusions showered on them by the ruling classes (political Islam is the most dramatic example of this). But from another angle, the rising movements of resistance and struggle against capitalism and imperialism across the five continents, the successes achieved, up to and including their electoral terms, by the new Left forces in Latin America (regardless of the limitations of these victories), the gradual radicalization of many of these movements, the initiation of critical positions taken by governments in the South within the WTO, are the proof that "another world," a better one, is becoming possible.

The offensive strategy necessary to rebuild the front of the peoples of the South demands the radicalization of social resistance against the offensive of imperialist capitalism. It requires their politicization in the fullest sense of the term, that is, their capacity to bring about the convergence of the struggles of peasants, women, workers, the unemployed, informal workers, and democratic intellectuals in order to set democratization and social progress as indissoluble objectives for the popular movement as a whole, which is possible in the immediate and longer terms. It requires that the values that lend legitimacy to this movement be of universal import (thus, that they be part of a socialist perspective) which, consequently, might even make it possible to overcome the divisions among the peoples of the South (between Muslims and Hindus, for example). Para-religious (political Islam, political Hinduism) or para-ethnic culturalisms are not possible allies in the fight for the emergence of an anti-imperialist alternative. On the contrary, they are the fundamentally reactionary allies of the forces that dominate the imperialist system. It cannot be ruled out that the mobilizations and advances that popular struggles can produce may succeed in modifying the policies implemented by the current governments in the countries of the South, and perhaps even impose positive changes in the nature of these governments. The beginning of such reorientations is already visible, as shown by the formation of the group of twenty and the group of ninety-nine within the WTO (regardless of the implicit ambiguities in these embodiments of diverse interests, convergent or divergent as the case may be).

The ruling classes of certain countries of the South have visibly opted for another strategy, which is neither passive submission to the dominant forces in the world system nor sworn opposition to the latter. Instead, they have implemented a strategy of active interventions on which they are basing their hope to speed up the development of their countries.

China was better equipped than others to make this choice and has derived from it incontestably brilliant results because of the solidity of the national construction produced by its revolution and Maoism, its choice to maintain control of its money and capital flows, and its refusal to call into question collective property (the principal revolutionary gain of the peasantry). Can the experience be continued? What are its possible limits? Analysis of the contradictions inherent in this option have led me to the conclusion that pursuing the project of a national capitalism capable of achieving equality with the major powers of the world system would be to revel in great illusions. The objective conditions inherited from history do not allow the implementation of a social historical compromise between capital, labor, and the peasantry that would guarantee the stability of the system. Consequently, such a system can ultimately only drift to the right (and thus be confronted with growing social movements of the working classes) or move to the left by constructing "market socialism" as a step on the long transition to socialism.

The apparently analogous choices made by the ruling classes of other so-called emergent countries are even more fragile. Neither Brazil nor India, because they have not made a radical revolution like China, are capable of resisting with as much force the combined pressures of imperialism and local reactionary classes. The winning over of these two governments to the global liberalism implemented by the WTO (at Hong Kong in December 2005) incontestably helped imperialism to avoid the disaster that had become apparent for it and dealt a hard blow to the beginning of an emerging front of the countries of the South. This huge error, while it is no longer serious, only serves the interests of the most reactionary local classes (the large landowners of Brazil and India) that are the natural allies of imperialism and certain enemies of the working classes in the countries concerned. The hopes that a portion of the historic Left of Latin America have invested in the social-democratic model are based on a huge error in judgment: social democracy could achieve what it did in Europe because it could be social-imperialist, which is what the conditions of Brazil or any other country in the South do not permit. The Sao Paulo Forum, which brought together the parties of the democratic Left in Latin America, certainly contributed positively to the democratic victories won by the peoples of the region over the course of the latest decades. Nevertheless, it also contributed to strengthening, here and there, social-democratic illusions.

TOWARD A FIFTH INTERNATIONAL?

The proposals that I am advancing imply a thorough preliminary analysis of what I have called the "political cultures" of different peoples. Political cultures are the combined product of the social, political, and ideological struggles in the history of the peoples concerned and the specific forms of their integration into globalized modernity. They are, consequently, specific and diverse, despite the common basis these nations share by belonging to the capitalist world. I have, among other things, emphasized the considerable distance that separates the political cultures of Europe, marked to various degrees by the French and Russian Revolutions, from the political culture of the United States, which has essentially disregarded those revolutions.

The globalization of the strategies of dominant capital calls for a global response by its victims. Then why not devise a new International that can provide an effective framework for the construction of the unity necessary for the success of the struggles undertaken by peoples against capital?

The response that I give to this question is affirmative, without hesitation, but on condition that the International under consideration be devised as the First one was and not the Second, Third, or Fourth. In other words, a new International Association of Workers open to all those who want to work together to construct convergence in diversity. Socialism (or communism) is, in this spirit, conceived as the product of the movement, not deduced from a preliminary definition. This proposal does not preclude the formulation of theoretical concepts concerning the society that it is desirable to build. On the contrary, it calls for them to be formulated with as much precision as possible, but it does rule out that one of them should be given a monopoly over defining the correct line and the steps of the transition.

The implementation of these principles of democracy will certainly be difficult, precisely because the exercise of democracy always is. It will indeed be necessary to set borders, agree that the definition of strategic objectives implies making choices, and that the correct management of the relation of a majority to a minority (or several minorities) is never given in advance.

I will not attempt, then, to offer responses to these questions, which, by definition, would contradict the principles I just formulated. I will instead propose several major objectives for strategies of struggle that could be effective responses to the current challenges. I will arrange these proposals into three groups:

1. Defeat liberalism at all levels, from the national to the global. This objective implies the restoration of the sovereign rights of peoples, recognition of this inherently fundamental and inalienable right and condemnation of the imperialist/colonial conception of global liberal management. Proposals for near-term objectives are possible within this perspective, such as the exclusion of agriculture from the WTO agenda, the abrogation of decisions imposed by the imperialist powers concerning intellectual and industrial property rights, the abrogation of decisions that hinder the development of non-market methods of managing natural resources and public services, the abrogation of prohibitions on regulating capital movements, the proclamation of the right of states to repudiate debts that, after an audit, turn out to be immoral or unsupportable, etc. At the national level, it seems possible to pass from the defensive to the offensive against all forms of insecurity in the conditions of workers that liberalism set up over the course of the last three decades. The revolt against the *Contrat première embauche*[19] in France is proof of this.

2. Defeat the plan for military control of the planet by the military forces of the United States and NATO. This objective entails unreserved condemnation of the repudiation of international law by the United States and the authorization it has given to itself to conduct preventive wars of choice and restoration of the United Nations to its proper functions. It entails the unconditional and immediate retreat of the armies of occupation in Iraq and the Israeli administration in Palestine and the dismantling of all the American military bases dispersed over every continent. Insofar as this project for control of the planet is not defeated morally, diplomatically, politically, and militarily, all democratic and social advances that the struggles of peoples might achieve would remain vulnerable, threatened with bombing by the U.S. Air Force.

3. Defeat in Europe of the liberal and Atlanticist conceptions that form the foundation of European Union institutions. That implies calling into question, from top to bottom, the entire construction of European institutions and the dissolution of NATO.

Initiatives have already been taken in the direction of specifying objectives for convergence strategies that correspond to the general view of the challenge proposed here. The conference organized at Bamako on January 18, 2006, on the eve of the opening of the 2006 Polycentric World Social Forum (Bamako and Caracas), was devoted precisely to discussing these proposals for strategies of struggle and constructing convergence in diversity. That this was possible and had significant results is undoubtedly an illustration that the world social movement, as it is called, is well and truly moving in this direction.

The objective of the Fifth International suggested here or, more modestly, the action and strategy proposals of the Bamako Appeal (see Appendix 2) is to contribute to the construction of the internationalism of peoples. Note that the phrase refers to all peoples, North and South, just as it refers not only to the proletariat but to all working classes and strata that are victims of the system, to humanity as a whole, threatened in its survival. This internationalism does not preclude strengthening the solidarity of the peoples of the three continents (Asia, Africa, Latin America) against aggression from the imperialism of the triad. On the contrary, these two internationalisms can only complement and reinforce each other. The solidarity of the peoples of the North and South cannot be based on charity, but on joint action against imperialism.

Strengthening the internationalism of peoples will create favorable conditions for facilitating advances in three directions that, combined closely together and not taken separately, build the alternative: social progress, the deepening of democracy, and the consolidation of national autonomy within a negotiated globalization.

Who can subscribe to this perspective? At this point, recall the question of "borders" referred to above. The Fifth International should not be an assembly exclusively of political parties, but should gather all peoples' movements of resistance and struggle and guarantee both their voluntary participation in the construction of joint strategies and the independence of their own decision making. Given that, there is certainly no cause to exclude once and for all political parties (or fractions of them) that, whether or not one wants to accept it, are important rallying points in the activities of civil society.

The fundamental principle can be formulated in the following two complementary expressions: no socialism without democracy (and thus no progress in the direction of socialism without the democratic practices of those who are actively working for this goal); and no democratic progress if it is not associated with social progress. Socialism must combine, and not only reconcile, aspirations to liberty and equality. This is a difficult combination in our era with the explosion of unbridled individualist ambitions encouraged by the capitalist system, accompanied by the abandonment of the objective of equality for which the questionable notion of "equality of opportunities" is substituted.

It is then possible to imagine that the political and social forces that find their natural place in this perspective are far from being reduced to a few small extremist political groups and NGOs of goodwill? Many of the large movements of struggle (the unions, associations of peasants, of women and of citizens) know from experience that there is strength in unity. The parties of the Third and Fourth Internationals should also find their place within this perspective, if they give up the idea of acting as self-proclaimed vanguards. Many democratic, social, and anti-imperialist parties on the peripheries will certainly understand that they could derive great advantages from the coordination of anti-imperialist struggles. But also unquestionably, the parties of the Second International who have been won over to liberalism and Atlanticism have excluded themselves from this perspective.

There is no question of going further in identifying the conditions for membership (analogous with the celebrated list of twenty-one conditions imposed on membership in the Third International). Serious debates on these principles and on the statutes of the International are indispensable. We appeal only for this process to begin.

The idea of a Fifth International has opponents and will have more if it becomes a reality. The opponents in question are, moreover, already associated with the World Social Forum and will devote themselves to maintaining that organization in a state of maximum powerlessness. The ideological proposals by which they plan to legitimize the inertia they suggest are well known. There is the attempt to establish equivalence between the diversity represented in the Forum and the self-proclaimed diversity of the plural Left (mainly in Europe). There is also the effort to take up the ideological thesis of "apolitical civil society" (or even anti-political civil society). This thesis is not new. It has always characterized the political culture of the United States. It carries some attraction for a number of NGOs formed over the course of the last few decades.

The objectives of these opponents are well known: it is a question of making the World Social Forum the complement of Davos. In other words, it is a question of not calling into question the fundamental principles of liberalism, capitalism, and imperialist globalization but of giving them a new legitimacy by allowing for minimum social demands (of the "fight against poverty" type). An association of so-called civil society organizations (as apolitical as possible) is deemed to be useful for formulating such demands. There are already initiatives set up for this purpose, supported by the Davos establishment, the G7, large foundations in the United States, and institutions of the European Union. The Mediterranean Forum (the so-called Barcelona initiative that is promoted by the European Union), the Arab Forum for Democracy (which has become the Forum for the Future) promoted by North American agencies, coalitions of select NGOs formed at the initiative of international institutions (mainly, the UN and World Bank) to follow up the large conferences organized by the institutions of the system (WTO and others) are all probably part of the attempt to divide the Social Forums, maybe cause them to fail or at least to ruin their potential to develop, become stronger and be effectively radicalized.

In contrast, the World Social Forum will certainly be counted among the friends of this International, if it ever comes into existence. The democratic principles on which the Fifth

International is to be based and the welcoming of all those who agree with its charter will allow members of this new International, as well as other organizations that desire to contribute to constructing convergence in diversity, without however, embracing to the socialist perspective, and organizations that decide to remain outside of the debates on joint strategy, to cohabit without problems. This diversity, which is the strength of the movement—despite the limiting effects of its dispersion—must be preserved.

APPENDIX 1

POLITICAL ISLAM IN THE SERVICE OF IMPERIALISM

All currents that claim adherence to political Islam proclaim the "specificity of Islam." According to them, Islam knows nothing of the separation between politics and religion, something supposedly distinctive of Christianity. It would accomplish nothing to remind them, as I have done, that their remarks reproduce, almost word for word, what European reactionaries at the beginning of the nineteenth century (such as de Bonald and de Maistre) said to condemn the rupture that the Enlightenment and the French Revolution had produced in the history of the Christian West!

On this basis, every current of political Islam chooses to conduct its struggle on the terrain of culture—but "culture" reduced in actual fact to the conventional affirmation of belonging to a particular religion. In reality, the militants of political Islam are not truly interested in discussing the dogmas that form religion. The ritual assertion of membership in the community is their exclusive preoccupation. Such a vision of the modern world is not only distressing because of the immense emptiness of thought that it conceals, but it also justifies imperialism's strategy of substituting a so-called conflict of cultures for the one between the imperialist centers and the dominated peripheries. The exclusive emphasis on culture allows political Islam to eliminate from every sphere of life the real social confrontations between the working classes and the global capitalist system that oppresses and exploits them. The militants of political Islam have no real presence in the areas where actual social conflict takes place and their leaders repeat incessantly that such conflicts are unimportant. Islamists are only present in these areas to open schools and health clinics. However, these are nothing but works of charity and means for indoctrination. They are not means of support for the struggles of the working classes against the system responsible for their poverty.

On the terrain of the real social issues, political Islam aligns itself with the camp of dependent capitalism and dominant imperialism. It defends the principle of the sacred character of property and legitimizes inequality and all the requirements of capitalist reproduction. The support by the Muslim Brotherhood in the Egyptian Parliament for the recent reactionary laws that reinforce the rights of property owners to the detriment of the rights of tenant farmers (the majority of the small peasantry) is but one example among hundreds of others. There is no example of even one reactionary law promoted in any Muslim state to which the Islamist movements are opposed. Moreover, such laws are promulgated with the agreement of the leaders of the imperialist system. Political Islam is not anti-imperialist, even if its militants think otherwise. It is an invaluable ally for imperialism and the latter knows it. It is easy to understand, then, that political Islam has always counted in its ranks the ruling classes of Saudi Arabia and Pakistan. Moreover, these classes were among its most active promoters from the very beginning. The local comprador bourgeoisies, the *nouveaux riches*, beneficiaries of current imperialist globalization, generously support political Islam. The latter has renounced an anti-imperialist perspective and substituted for it an anti-Western (almost anti-Christian) position, which only leads the societies concerned into an impasse and hence does not form an obstacle to the deployment of imperialist control over the world system.

Political Islam is not only reactionary on certain questions (notably, the status of women) and is perhaps even responsible for fanatical excesses directed against non-Muslim citizens (such as the Copts in Egypt). It is fundamentally reactionary and therefore obviously cannot participate in the progress of peoples' liberation.

Three major arguments are nevertheless advanced to encourage social movements as a whole to enter into dialogue with the movements of political Islam. The first is that political Islam mobilizes numerous popular masses, which is something that cannot be ignored or scorned. Numerous images certainly reinforce this claim. Still, one should keep a cool head and properly assess the "mobilizations" in question. The electoral "successes" that have been organized are put into perspective as soon as they are subjected to more rigorous analyses. For example, the huge proportion of abstentions—more than 75 percent—in the Egyptian elections. The power of the Islamist street is, in large part, simply the reverse side of the weaknesses of the organized Left, which is absent from the spheres in which current social conflicts are occurring.

Even if it were agreed that political Islam actually "mobilizes" significant numbers, does that justify concluding that the Left must seek to include political Islamic organizations in alliances for political or social action? If political Islam successfully mobilizes large numbers of people, that is simply a fact, and any effective political strategy must include this fact in its considerations, proposals and options. But seeking alliances is not necessarily the best means to deal with this challenge. (Should—or could, moreover—Nazi or fascist masses have been included in a common front?). It should be pointed out that the organizations of political Islam—the Muslim Brotherhood in particular—are not seeking such an alliance, indeed they even reject it. If some unfortunate Leftist organizations come to believe that political Islamic organizations have accepted them, the first decision the latter would make, after having succeeded in coming to power, would be to liquidate their burdensome ally with extreme violence, as was the case in Iran with the Mujahideen and the Fidayeen Khalq.[20]

The second reason put forward by the partisans of "dialogue" is that political Islam, even if it is reactionary in terms of social proposals, is anti-imperialist. I have heard it said that the criterion that I propose (unreserved support for struggles carried out for social progress) is "economistic" and neglects the political dimensions of the challenge that confronts the peoples of the South. I do not believe that this critique is valid given what I have said about the democratic and national dimensions of the desirable responses for handling this challenge. I also agree that in their response to the challenge, the forces in action are not necessarily consistent in their manner of dealing with its social and political dimensions. It is thus possible to imagine a political Islam that is anti-imperialist, though regressive on the social plane. Iran, Hamas in Palestine, Hezbollah in Lebanon, and certain resistance movements in Iraq immediately come to mind. I will discuss these particular situations later. What I contend is that political Islam as a whole is quite simply not anti-imperialist but is altogether lined up behind the dominant powers on the world scene.

The third argument calls the attention of the Left to the necessity of combating Islamophobia. Any Left worthy of the name cannot ignore the *question des banlieues*;[21] that is, the treatment of the popular classes of immigrant origin in the metropolises of contemporary developed capitalism. Analysis of this challenge and the responses provided by various groups (the interested parties themselves, the European electoral Left, the radical Left) lies outside the focus of this text. I will content myself with expressing my viewpoint in principle: the progressive response cannot be based on the institutionalization of communitarianism, which is essentially and necessarily always associated with inequality and ultimately originates in a racist culture. A specific product of the reactionary political culture of the United States, communitarianism (already triumphant in Great Britain) is beginning to pollute political life on the European continent. Islamophobia, systematically promoted by important sections of the political elite and the media, is part of a strategy for managing community diversity for capital's benefit, because this supposed respect for diversity is, in fact, only the means to deepen divisions within the popular classes.

The question of the so-called problem neighborhoods (*banlieues*) is specific, and confusing it with the question of imperialism (i.e., the imperialist management of the relations between the dominant imperialist centers and the dominated peripheries), as is sometimes done, will contribute nothing to making progress on each of these completely distinct terrains. This confusion is part of the reactionary toolbox and reinforces Islamphobia, which, in turn, makes it possible to legitimize both the offensive against the popular classes in the imperialist centers and the offensive against the peoples of the peripheries. This confusion and Islamophobia, in turn, provide a valuable service to reactionary political Islam, giving credibility to its anti-Western discourse. I say, then, that the two reactionary ideological campaigns promoted by the racist Right in the West and by political Islam mutually support each other, just as they support communitarian practices.

MODERNITY, DEMOCRACY, SECULARISM, AND ISLAM

The image that the Arab and Islamic regions give of themselves today is that of societies in which religion (Islam) is at the forefront in all areas of social and political life, to the point that it appears strange to imagine that it could be different. The majority of foreign observers (political leaders and the media) conclude that modernity, perhaps even democracy, will have to adapt to the strong presence of Islam, *de facto* precluding secularism. Either this reconciliation is possible and it will be necessary to support it or it is not possible and it will be necessary to deal with this region of the world as it is. I do not at all share this so-called realist vision. The future—in the long view of a global socialism—is, for the peoples of this region as for others, democracy and secularism. Such a future is possible in these regions as elsewhere, but nothing is guaranteed and certain anywhere.

Modernity is a rupture in world history, initiated in Europe during the sixteenth century. Modernity proclaims that human beings are responsible for their own history, individually and collectively, and consequently breaks with the dominant premodern ideologies. Modernity, then, makes democracy possible, just as it requires secularism, in the sense of separation of the religious and the political. Formulated by the eighteenth-century Enlightenment, and implemented by the French Revolution, the complex association of modernity, democracy, and secularism, its advances and retreats, has been shaping the contemporary world ever since. But modernity by itself is not only a cultural revolution. It derives its meaning only through the close relation that it has with the birth and subsequent growth of capitalism. This relation has conditioned the historic limits of "really existing" modernity. The concrete forms of democracy and secularism found today must, then, be considered as products of the concrete history of the growth of capitalism. They are shaped by the specific conditions in which the domination of capital is expressed—the historical compromises that define the social contents of hegemonic blocs (what I call the historical course of political cultures).

This condensed presentation of my understanding of the historical materialist method is evoked here simply to situate the diverse ways of combining capitalist modernity, democracy, and secularism in their theoretical context.

The Enlightenment and the French Revolution put forward a model of radical secularism. Atheist or agnostic, deist or believer (in this case Christian), the individual is free to choose and the state is indifferent to that choice. On the European continent—and in France beginning with the Restoration—the retreats and compromises that combined the power of the bourgeoisie with that of the dominant classes of the pre-modern systems were the basis for attenuated forms of secularism, understood as a form of tolerance that does not exclude the social role of the Churches from the polity. As for the United States, its particular historical path resulted in the formation of a fundamentally reactionary political culture, in which genuine secularism is practically unknown. Religion here is a recognized social actor and secularism is confused with the multiplicity of official religions (any religion—or even sect—is official).

There is an obvious link between the degree of radical secularism upheld and the degree of support for shaping society in accord with the central theme of modernity. The Left, be it radical or even moderate, which believes in the effectiveness of politics to orient social evolution in chosen directions, defends strong concepts of secularism. The conservative Right claims that things should be allowed to evolve on their own whether the question is economic, political, or social. As to the economy, the choice in favor of the "market" is obviously favorable to capital. In politics, "low-intensity democracy" becomes the rule, "alternation" is substituted for alternative. And in society, in this context, politics has no need for active secularism—"communities" compensate for the deficiencies of the state. The market and representative democracy make history and they should be allowed to do so. In the current moment of the Left's retreat, this conservative version of social thought is widely dominant, in formulations that run the gamut from those of Alain Touraine to those of Antonio Negri. The reactionary political culture of the United States goes even further in negating the responsibility of political action. The assertion that God inspires the American nation, and the adherence to this belief, reduce the concept of secularism to nothing. To say that God makes history is to allow the market alone to do it.

From this point of view, where are the peoples of the Middle East region situated? The image of bearded men bowed low and groups of veiled women give rise to hasty conclusions about the intensity of religious adherence among individuals. The social pressures exercised to obtain certain behaviors are rarely mentioned. Women have not chosen the veil; it has been imposed on them with violence. If absence from prayer is noticed, the result is almost always loss of work, some times even loss of life. Western "culturalist" friends who call for respect for the diversity of beliefs rarely find out about the procedures implemented by the authorities to present an image that is convenient for them. There are certainly those who are "crazy for God" (*fous de Dieu*). Are they proportionally more numerous than the Spanish Catholics who march on Easter? Or the vast crowds who listen to televangelists in the United States?

In any case, the region has not always projected this image of itself. Beyond the differences from country to country, a large region can be identified that runs from Morocco to Afghanistan, including all the Arab peoples (with the exception of those in the Arabian peninsula), the Turks, Iranians, Afghans, and peoples of the former Soviet Central Asian republics, in which the possibilities for the development of secularism are far from negligible. The situation is different among other neighboring peoples, the Arabs of the peninsula or the Pakistanis.

In this region, political traditions have been strongly marked by the radical currents of modernity: the ideas of the Enlightenment, the French Revolution, the Russian Revolution, and the communism of the Third International were present in the minds of everyone and were much more important than the parliamentarianism of Westminster, for example. These dominant currents inspired the major models for political transformation implemented by the ruling classes, which could be described, in some of their aspects, as forms of enlightened despotism.

This was certainly the case in the Egypt of Mohammed Ali or Khedive Ismail. Kemalism in Turkey and modernization in Iran were similar. The national populism of more recent stages of history belongs to the same family of modernist political projects. The variants of the model were numerous (the Algerian, National Liberation Front, Tunisian Bourguibism, Egyptian Nasserism, the Baathism of Syria and Iraq), but the direction of movement was analogous. Apparently extreme experiences—the so-called communist regimes in Afghanistan and South Yemen—were really not very different. All of these regimes accomplished much and had wide popular support. This is why, even though they were not truly democratic, they opened the way to a possible development in this direction. In certain circumstances, such as those in Egypt from 1920 to 1950, an experiment in electoral democracy was attempted, supported by the moderate anti-imperialist center (the Wafd party), opposed by the dominant imperialist power (Great Britain) and its local allies (the monarchy). Secularism, implemented in a moderate version, to be sure, was not refused by the people. On the contrary, religious people were regarded as obscurantists by general public opinion, and most of them were.

The modernist experiments, from enlightened despotism to radical national populism, were not products of chance. Powerful movements that were dominant in the middle classes created them. In this way, these classes expressed their will to be viewed as fully-fledged partners in modern globalization. These projects, which can be described as national bourgeois, were modernist, secularizing, and potential carriers of democratic developments. But precisely because these projects conflicted with the interests of dominant imperialism, the latter fought them relentlessly and systematically mobilized declining obscurantist forces for this purpose.

The history of the Muslim Brotherhood is well known. It was literally created in the 1920s by the British and the monarchy to block the path of the democratic and secular Wafd. Their mass return from their Saudi refuge after Gamal Abdel Nasser's death, organized by the CIA and Sadat, is also well known. We are all acquainted with the history of the Taliban, formed by the CIA in Pakistan to fight the "communists" who had opened the schools to everyone, boys and girls. It is even well known that the Israelis supported Hamas at the beginning in order to weaken the secular and democratic currents of the Palestinian resistance.

Political Islam would have had much more difficulty in moving out from the borders of Saudi Arabia and Pakistan without the continual, powerful, and resolute support of the United States. Saudi Arabian society had not even begun its move out of tradition when petroleum was discovered under its soil. An alliance between imperialism and the traditional ruling class was sealed immediately, and it gave a new lease on life to Wahabi political Islam. On their side, the British succeeded in breaking Indian unity by persuading the Muslim leaders to create their own state, trapped from its birth in political Islam. It should be noted that the theory by which this curiosity was legitimated—attributed to Mawdudi[22]—had been completely drawn up beforehand by the English Orientalists in His Majesty's service.

It is thus easy to understand the initiative taken by the United States to break the united front of Asian and African states set up at Bandung (1955) by creating an Islamic Conference, immediately promoted (from 1957) by Saudi Arabia and Pakistan. Political Islam penetrated into the region by this means.

The least of the conclusions that should be drawn from the observations made here is that political Islam is not the spontaneous result of the assertion of authentic religious convictions by the peoples concerned. Political Islam was constructed by the systematic action of imperialism, supported, of course, by obscurantist reactionary forces and subservient comprador classes. That this state of affairs is also the responsibility of Left forces that neither saw nor knew how to deal with the challenge remains indisputable.

QUESTIONS RELATIVE TO THE FRONT LINE COUNTRIES: AFGHANISTAN, IRAQ, PALESTINE, IRAN

The project of the United States, supported to varying degrees by their allies in Europe and Japan, is to establish military control over the entire planet. With this prospect in mind, the Middle East was chosen as the "first strike" region for four reasons: 1. it holds the most abundant petroleum resources in the world and its direct control by the armed forces of the United States would give Washington a privileged position, placing its allies—Europe and Japan—and possible rivals (China) in an uncomfortable position of dependence for their energy supplies; 2. it is located at the crossroads of the Old World and makes it easier to put in place a permanent military threat against China, India, and Russia; 3. the region is experiencing a moment of weakness and confusion that allows the aggressor to be assured of an easy victory, at least for the moment; and 4. Israel's presence in the region—Washington's unconditional ally.

This aggression has placed the countries and nations located on the front line (Afghanistan, Iraq, Palestine, Iran) in the particular situation of being destroyed (the first three) or threatened with destruction (Iran).

AFGHANISTAN

Afghanistan experienced the best period in its modern history during the so-called communist republic. This was a regime of modernist enlightened despotism that opened up the educational system to children of both sexes. It was an enemy of obscurantism and, for this reason, had decisive support within the society. The agrarian reform it had undertaken was, for the most part, a group of measures intended to reduce the tyrannical powers of tribal leaders. The support—at least tacit—of the majority of the peasantry guaranteed the probable success of this promising change. The propaganda conveyed by the Western media as well as by political Islam presented this experiment as communist and atheist totalitarianism that was rejected by the Afghan people. In reality, the regime was far from being unpopular, much like Ataturk in his time.

The fact that the leaders of this experiment, in both of the major factions (Khalq and Parcham), were self-described as communists is not surprising. The model of progress accomplished by the neighboring peoples of Soviet Central Asia (despite everything that has been said on the subject and despite the autocratic practices of the system) in comparison with the ongoing social disasters of British imperialist management in other neighboring countries (India and Pakistan included) had the effect, here as in many other countries of the region, of encouraging patriots to assess the full extent of the obstacle formed by imperialism to any attempt at modernization. The invitation extended by one faction to the Soviets to intervene in order to rid themselves of the others certainly had a negative effect and mortgaged the possibilities of the modernist national populist project.

The United States in particular and allies of the triad in general have always been tenacious opponents of the Afghan modernizers, communists or not. It is they who mobilized the obscurantist forces of Pakistan-style political Islam (the Taliban) and the warlords (the tribal leaders successfully neutralized by the so-called communist regime) and then trained and armed them. Even after the Soviet retreat, the Najibullah government demonstrated the capability for resistance. It probably would have gained the upper hand but for the Pakistani military offensive that came to support the Taliban and the offensive of the reconstituted forces of the warlords, which increased the chaos.

Afghanistan was devastated by the intervention of the United States and its allies and agents, the Islamists in particular. Afghanistan cannot be reconstructed under their authority, barely disguised behind a clown without roots in the country, who was parachuted there by the Texas transnational by whom he was employed. The supposed "democracy," in the name of which Washington, NATO, and the UN, claim to justify the continuation of their presence (in fact, occupation), was a lie from the very beginning and has become a huge farce.

There is only one solution to the Afghan problem: all foreign forces should leave the country and all powers should be forced to refrain from financing and arming their allies. To those who are well intended and express their fear that the Afghan people will then tolerate the dictatorship of the Taliban (or the warlords), I would respond that the foreign presence has been up until now and remains the best support for this dictatorship. The Afghan people had been moving in another direction—potentially the best possible—at a time when the West was forced to take less interest in its affairs. To the enlightened despotism of "communists," the civilized West has always preferred obscurantist despotism, infinitely less dangerous for its interests.

IRAQ

The armed diplomacy of the United States had the objective of literally destroying Iraq well before pretexts were actually given to it to do so on two different occasions: the invasion of Kuwait in 1990 and then after September 11, 2001—exploited for this purpose by Bush with Goebbels-style cynicism and lies ("If you tell a lie big enough and keep repeating it, people will eventually come to believe it"). The reason is simple and has nothing to do with the discourse calling for the liberation of the Iraqi people from the bloody dictatorship (real enough) of Saddam Hussein. Iraq possesses a large part of the best petroleum resources on the planet. But, what is more, Iraq had succeeded in training scientific and technical cadres that were capable, through their critical mass, of supporting a coherent and substantial national project. This danger had to be eliminated by a preventive war that the United States gave itself the right to carry out when and where it decided, without the least respect for international law.

Beyond this obviously observation, several serious questions should be examined: 1. How could Washington's plan appear to be such a dazzling success so easily?; 2. What new situation has been created and confronts the Iraqi nation today?; 3. What responses are the various elements of the Iraqi population giving to this challenge?; and 4. What solutions can the democratic and progressive Iraqi, Arab, and international forces promote?

Saddam Hussein's defeat was predictable. Faced with an enemy whose main advantage lies in its capability to effect genocide with impunity by aerial bombardment (the use of nuclear weapons is to come), the people have only one possible effective response: carry out resistance on their invaded territory. Saddam's regime was devoted to eliminating every means of defense within reach of its people through the systematic destruction of any organization and every political party (beginning with the Communist Party) that had been involved in making the history of modern Iraq, including the Baath itself, which had been one of the major actors in this history. It is not surprising in these conditions that the Iraqi people allowed their country to be invaded without a struggle, nor even that some developments (such as the apparent participation in elections organized by the invader or the outburst of fratricidal fighting among Kurds, Sunni Arabs and Shia Arabs) seemed to be signs of a possible accepted defeat (on which Washington had based its calculations). But what is worthy of note is that the resistance on the ground grows stronger every day (despite all of the serious weaknesses displayed by the various resistance forces), that it has already made it impossible to establish a regime of lackeys capable of maintaining the appearance of order; and in a way, that it has already demonstrated the failure of Washington's project.

A new situation has, nevertheless, been created by the foreign military occupation. The Iraqi nation is truly threatened. Washington is incapable of maintaining its control over the country (so as to pillage its petroleum resources, which is its number one objective) through the intermediary of a seemingly national government. The only way it can continue its project, then, is to break the country apart. The division of the country into at least three states (Kurd, Sunni Arab, and Shia Arab) was, perhaps from the very beginning, Washington's objective, in alignment with Israel (the archives will reveal the truth of that in the future). Today, the "civil war" is the card that Washington plays to legitimize the continuation of its occupation. Clearly, permanent occupation was—and remains—the objective: it is the only means by which Washington can guarantee its control of the petroleum resources. Certainly, no credence can be given to Washington's declarations of intent, such as "We will leave the country as soon as order has been restored." It should be remembered that the British never said of their occupation of Egypt, beginning in 1882, that it was anything other than provisional (it lasted until 1956!). Meanwhile, of course, the United States destroys the country—its schools, factories, and scientific capacities—a little more each day, using all means, including the most criminal.

The responses given by the Iraqi people to the challenge—so far, at least—do not appear to be up to facing the seriousness of the situation. That is the least that can be said. What are the reasons for this? The dominant Western media repeat *ad nauseam* that Iraq is an "artificial" country and that the oppressive domination of Saddam's "Sunni" regime over the Shia and Kurds is the origin of the inevitable civil war (which can only be suppressed, perhaps, by continuing the foreign occupation). The resistance, then, is limited to a few pro-Saddam hard-core Islamists from the Sunni triangle. It is surely difficult to string together so many falsehoods.

Following the First World War, the British had great difficulty in defeating the resistance of the Iraqi people. In complete harmony with their imperial tradition, the British imported a monarchy and created a class of large landowners to support their power, thereby giving a privileged position to the Sunnis. But, despite their systematic efforts, the British failed. The Communist

Party and the Baath Party were the main organized political forces that defeated the power of the "Sunni" monarchy detested by everyone Sunni, Shia, and Kurd. The violent competition between these two forces, which occupied center stage between 1958 and 1963, ended up with the victory of the Baath Party, welcomed at the time by the Western powers as a relief. However, the Communist project carried in itself the possibility for a democratic evolution; this was not true of the Baath. The latter was nationalist and pan-Arab in principle, admired the Prussian model for constructing German unity, and recruited its members from the secular, modernist petite bourgeoisie hostile to obscurantist expressions of religion. In power, the Baath evolved, in predictable fashion, into a dictatorship whose state socialism was only half anti-imperialist, in the sense that, depending on conjunctures and circumstances, a compromise could be accepted by the two partners (Baathist power in Iraq and American imperialism, dominant in the region). This deal encouraged the megalomaniacal excesses of the leader, who imagined that Washington would accept making him its main ally in the region. Washington's support for Baghdad (the delivery of chemical weapons is proof of this) in the absurd and criminal war against Iran from 1980 to 1989 appeared to lend credence to this calculation. Saddam never imagined that Washington had cheated, that modernization of Iraq was unacceptable to imperialism and that the decision to destroy the country had already been taken. Saddam fell into the open trap when the green light was given to annex Kuwait (in fact, attached in Ottoman times to the provinces that constitute Iraq, and detached by the British in order to make it one of their petroleum colonies). Iraq was then subjected to ten years of sanctions intended to bleed the country dry so as to facilitate the glorious conquest of the resulting vacuum by the armed forces of the United States.

The successive Baathist regimes, including the last one in its declining phase under Saddam's leadership, can be accused of everything, except for having stirred up the conflict between the Sunni and Shia. Who then is responsible for the bloody clashes between the two communities? One day, we will certainly learn how the CIA (and undoubtedly Mossad) organized many of these massacres. But, beyond that, it is true that the political desert created by the Saddam regime and the example that it provided of unprincipled opportunist methods encouraged aspirants to power of all kinds to follow this path, often protected by the occupier. Sometimes, perhaps, they were even naïve to the point of believing that they could be of service to the occupying power. The aspirants in question, be they religious leaders (Shia or Sunni), supposed (para-tribal) notables or notoriously corrupt businessmen exported by the United States, never had any real political standing in the country. Even those religious leaders whom the believers respected had no political influence that was acceptable to the Iraqi people. Without the void created by Saddam, no one would know how to pronounce their names. Faced with the new political world created by the imperialism of liberal globalization will other authentically popular and national, possibly even democratic, political forces have the means to reconstruct themselves?

There was a time when the Iraqi Communist Party was the focus for organizing the best of what Iraqi society could produce. The Communist Party was established in every region of the country and dominated the world of intellectuals, often of Shia origin (I note in passing that the Shia produced revolutionaries or religious leaders above all, rarely bureaucrats or compradors). The Communist Party was authentically popular and anti-imperialist, little inclined to demagoguery and potentially democratic. After the massacre of thousands of its best militants by the Baathist dictatorships, the collapse of the Soviet Union (for which it was not prepared), and the behavior of those intellectuals who believed it acceptable to return from exile as camp followers of the armed forces of the United States, is it henceforth fated to disappear permanently from history? Unfortunately, this is all too possible, but not inevitable, far from it.

The Kurdish question is real, in Iraq as in Iran and Turkey. But on this subject also, it should be remembered that the Western powers have always practiced, with great cynicism, double standards. The repression of Kurdish demands has never attained in

Iraq and Iran the level of police, military, political, and moral violence carried out by Ankara. Neither Iran nor Iraq has ever gone so far as to deny the very existence of the Kurds. However, Turkey must be pardoned for everything as a member of NATO, an organization of democratic nations, as the media remind us. Among the eminent democrats was Antonio de Oliveira Salazar, one of the founding members, and those no less ardent admirers of democracy, the Greek colonels and Turkish generals.

Each time that the Iraqi popular fronts, formed around the Communist Party and the Baath in the best moments of its turbulent history, exercised political power, they always found an area of agreement with the principal Kurdish parties. The latter, moreover, have always been their allies.

The anti-Shia and anti-Kurd excesses of the Saddam regime were certainly real: for example, the bombing of the Basra region by Saddam's army after its defeat in Kuwait in 1990 and the use of gas against the Kurds. These excesses came in response to the maneuvers of Washington's armed diplomacy, which had mobilized sorcerer's apprentices to seize the opportunity. They remain no less criminal excesses, and stupid, moreover, since the success of Washington's appeals was quite limited. But can anything else be expected from dictators like Saddam?

The force of the resistance to foreign occupation, unexpected under these conditions, might seem to be miraculous. This is not the case, since the basic reality is that the Iraqi people as a whole (Arab and Kurd, Sunni and Shia) detest the occupier and are familiar with its crimes on a daily basis (assassinations, bombings, massacres, torture). Given this a united front of national resistance (call it what you want) might be imagined, proclaiming itself as such, posting the names, lists of organizations and parties composing it and their common program. This, however, is not actually the case up to the present, particularly for all the reasons described above, including the destruction of the social and political fabric of the country caused by the Saddam dictatorship and the occupation. Regardless of the reasons, this is a serious handicap, which makes it easier to divide the population, encourage opportunists, going so far as to make them collaborators, and throw confusion over the objectives of the liberation.

Who will succeed in overcoming these handicaps? The communists should be well placed to do so. Already, militants who are present on the ground are separating themselves from the leaders of the Communist Party (the only ones known by the dominant media) who, confused and embarrassed, are attempting to give a semblance of legitimacy to their rallying to the collaborationist government, even pretending that they are adding to the effectiveness of armed resistance by such action! But under the circumstances many other political forces could make decisive initiatives in the direction of forming this front.

It remains the case that, despite its weaknesses, the Iraqi people's resistance has already defeated (politically if not yet militarily) Washington's project. It is precisely this that worries the Atlanticists in the European Union, faithful allies of the United States. Today, they fear a U.S. defeat, because this would strengthen the capacity of the peoples of the South to force transnational capital of the imperialist triad to respect the interests of the nations and peoples of Asia, Africa, and Latin America.

The Iraqi resistance has offered proposals that would make it possible to get out of the impasse and aid the United States to withdraw from the trap. It proposes: 1. the formation of a transitional administrative authority set up with the support of the UN Security Council; 2. the immediate cessation of resistance actions and of military and police interventions by occupying forces; and 3. the departure of all foreign military and civilian authorities within six months. The details of these proposals have been published in the prestigious Arab review *Al Moustaqbal al Arabi* (January 2006), published in Beirut.

The absolute silence with which the European media oppose the dissemination of this message is a testament to the solidarity of the imperialist partners. Democratic and progressive European forces have the duty to dissociate themselves from this policy of the imperialist triad and support the proposals of the Iraqi resistance. To leave the Iraqi people to confront its opponent alone is not an acceptable option: it reinforces the dangerous idea that nothing can be expected from the West and its peoples, and consequently encourages the unacceptable—even criminal—excesses in the activities of some of the resistance movements.

The sooner the foreign occupation troops leave the country and the stronger the support by democratic forces in the world and in Europe for the Iraqi people, the greater the possibilities for a better future for this martyred people. The longer the occupation lasts, the more dismal will be the aftermath of its inevitable end.

PALESTINE

The Palestinian people have, since the Balfour Declaration during the First World War, been the victim of a colonization project by a foreign population, who reserve for them the fate of the "redskins," whether one acknowledges it or pretends to be ignorant of it. This project has always had the unconditional support of the dominant imperialist power in the region (yesterday Great Britain, today the United States), because the foreign state in the region formed by that project can only be the unconditional ally, in turn, of the interventions required to force the Arab Middle East to submit to the domination of imperialist capitalism.

This is an obvious fact for all the peoples of Africa and Asia. Consequently, on both continents they are spontaneously united in the assertion and defense of the rights of the Palestinian people. On the other hand, in Europe, the "Palestinian question" causes division, produced by the confusions kept alive by Zionist ideology, which is frequently echoed favorably.

Today more than ever, in conjunction with the implementation of the American Greater Middle East project, the rights of the Palestinian people have been abolished. All the same, the PLO accepted the Oslo and Madrid plans and the roadmap drafted by Washington. It is Israel that has openly gone back on its agreement, and implemented an even more ambitious expansion plan. The PLO has been undermined as a result: public opinion can justly reproach it with having naively believed in the sincerity of its adversaries. The support provided by the occupation authorities to its Islamist adversary (Hamas), in the beginning, at least, and the spread of corrupt practices in the Palestinian administration (on which the fund donors—the World Bank, Europe, NGOs—are silent, if they are not party to it) had to lead to the Hamas electoral victory (it was predictable and probably desirable). This then became an additional pretext immediately put forward to justify unconditional alignment with Israeli policies no matter what they may be.

The Zionist colonial project has always been a threat, beyond Palestine, for neighboring Arab peoples. Its ambitions to annex the Egyptian Sinai and its effective annexation of the Syrian Golan Heights are testimony to that. In the Greater Middle East project, a particular place is granted to Israel, to its regional monopoly of nuclear military equipment and its role as "indispensable partner" (under the fallacious pretext that Israel has technological expertise of which the Arab people are incapable—what an indispensable racism!).

It is not my intention here to offer analysis of the complex interactions between the resistance struggles against Zionist colonial expansion and the political conflicts and choices in Lebanon and Syria. The Baathist regimes in Syria have resisted, in their own way, the demands of the imperialist powers and Israel. That this resistance has also served to legitimize more questionable ambitions (control of Lebanon) is certainly not debatable. Moreover, Syria has carefully chosen the least dangerous allies in Lebanon. It is well known that the Lebanese Communist Party organized resistance to the Israeli incursions in South Lebanon (diversion of water included). The Syrian, Lebanese, and Iranian authorities closely cooperated to destroy this "dangerous base" and replace it with Hezbollah. The assassination of Rafiq al-Harriri (which is still an unresolved case) obviously gave the imperialist powers (the United States in front, France behind) the opportunity to intervene. They had two objectives in mind: 1. to force Damascus to align itself permanently with the vassal Arab states (Egypt and Saudi Arabia)—or, failing that, to eliminate the vestiges of a deteriorated Baathist power; and 2. to demolish what remains of the capability to resist Israeli incursions (by demanding the disarmament of Hezbollah). Rhetoric about democracy can be invoked within this context, if useful.

Today, to accept the implementation of the Israeli project in progress is to ratify the abolition of the primary right of peoples: the right to exist. This is the supreme crime against humanity. The accusation of "anti-Semitism" addressed to those who reject this crime is only a means for appalling blackmail.

IRAN

It is not my intention here to develop the analysis called for by the Islamic Revolution. Was it, as it has been proclaimed to be among supporters of political Islam as well as among foreign observers, the declaration of and point of departure for a change that ultimately will seize the entire region, perhaps even the whole Muslim world, renamed for the occasion the *umma* (the "nation," which has never been)? Or was it a singular event, a unique combination of interpretations of Shia Islam and the expression of Iranian nationalism?

From the perspective of what interests us here, I will only make two observations. The first is that the regime of political Islam in Iran is not by nature incompatible with integration of the country into the global capitalist system such as it is, since the regime is based on liberal principles for managing the economy. The second is that the Iranian nation as such is a "strong nation," one whose major components, in both the popular classes and ruling classes, do not accept the integration of their country into the global system in a dominated position. There is, of course, a contradiction between these two dimensions of the Iranian reality. The second one accounts for Teheran's foreign policy tendencies, which bear witness to the will to resist foreign diktats.

It is Iranian nationalism—powerful and, in my opinion, altogether historically positive—that explains the success of the modernization of scientific, industrial, technological, and military capabilities undertaken by the Shah's regime and the Khomeinist regime that followed. Iran is one of the few states of the South (along with China, India, Korea, Brazil, and maybe a few others, but not many) to have a national bourgeois project. Whether it be possible in the long term to achieve this project or not (my opinion is that it is not) is not the focus of our discussion. Today this project exists and is in place.

It is precisely because Iran forms a critical mass capable of attempting to assert itself as a respected partner that the United States has decided to destroy the country by a new preventive war. As is well known, the conflict is taking place around the nuclear capabilities that Iran is developing. Why should this country, just like others, not have the right to pursue these capabilities, up to and including becoming a nuclear military power? By what right can the imperialist powers and their Israeli accomplice boast about granting themselves a monopoly over weapons of mass destruction? Can one give any credit to the discourse that argues that democratic nations will never make use of such weapons like "rogue states" might, when it is common knowledge that the democratic nations in question are responsible for the greatest genocides of modern times, including the one against the Jews, and that the United States has already used atomic weapons and still today rejects an absolute and general ban on their use?

CONCLUSION

Today, three groups of forces are embroiled in political conflicts in the region: 1. those that proclaim their nationalist past (but are, in reality, nothing more than the degenerate and corrupt inheritors of the bureaucracies of the national-populist era); 2. those that proclaim political Islam; and 3. those that are attempting to organize around "democratic" demands that are compatible with economic liberalism. The consolidation of power by any of these forces is not acceptable to a Left that is attentive to the interests of the popular classes. In fact, the interests of the comprador classes affiliated with the current imperialist system are expressed through these three tendencies. American diplomacy keeps all three irons in the fire, since it is focused on using the conflicts among them for its exclusive benefit. For the Left to attempt to become involved in these conflicts through alliances with one or another of the tendencies (preferring the regimes in place to avoid the worst, i.e., political Islam or, on the other hand, seeking to be allied with the latter in order to get rid of the regimes) is doomed to fail. The Left must assert itself by undertaking struggles in areas where it finds its natural place: defense of the economic and social interests of the popular classes, democracy, and the assertion of national sovereignty, all viewed together as inseparable.

The region of the Greater Middle East is today central in the conflict between the imperialist leader and the peoples of the entire world. Defeat of the Washington establishment's project is the condition for providing the possibility of success for advances in any region of the world. Failing that, all these advances will remain vulnerable in the extreme. That does not mean that the importance of struggles carried out in other regions of the world, in Europe or Latin America or elsewhere, can be ignored. It means only that they should be part of a comprehensive perspective that contributes to defeating Washington in the region that it has chosen for its first criminal strike of this century.

APPENDIX 2

THE BAMAKO APPEAL[23]

I. INTRODUCTION

A new collective consciousness has arisen out of the experience of more than five years of worldwide gatherings of those who are resisting neoliberalism. The World, Thematic, Continental, and National Social Forums and the Assembly of Social Movements have been the principal architects of this consciousness. Meeting in Bamako on January 18, 2006, on the eve of the opening of the Polycentric World Social Forum, the participants in this special day dedicated to the fiftieth anniversary of the Bandung Conference have expressed the need to define other development objectives, create harmony in societies by abolishing exploitation by class, gender, race, and caste, and show the way to a new balance of power between the South and the North.

The Bamako Appeal aims to contribute to the emergence of a new popular and historical subject and to consolidate the gains made at these meetings. It seeks to promote the principle of the right of everyone to enjoy a full life, put forward the broad outlines of a collective life of peace, justice, and diversity, and advance ways of achieving these objectives at the local level and at the level of humanity as a whole.

In order for an historical subject to arise, one that is popular, diverse, and multipolar, it is necessary to define and promote alternatives capable of mobilizing social and political forces. The radical transformation of the capitalist system is the objective.

Capitalism's destruction of the planet and of millions of human beings, the individualistic culture of consumption that accompanies and supports it, and its imposition by imperialist forces are no longer acceptable because the very existence of humanity is at stake. Any alternatives must be based on the long tradition of popular resistance and also include the small steps forward that are indispensable to the daily life of capitalism's victims.

The Bamako Appeal, constructed around broad themes discussed in committees, expresses its commitment to:

(i) Construct an internationalism that joins the peoples of the South and North who are ravaged by the dictatorship of financial markets and the uncontrolled global expansion of transnational corporations;

(ii) Construct the solidarity of the peoples of Asia, Africa, Europe, and the Americas confronted with the challenges of development in the twenty-first century;

(iii) Construct a political, economic and cultural consensus that is an alternative to neoliberal and militarized globalization and the hegemony of the United States and its allies.

II. THE PRINCIPLES

1. Construct a world based on solidarity among human beings and peoples.

Our era is dominated by the imposition of competition between workers, nations, and peoples. However, the principle of solidarity has, historically, played a role far more conducive to the effective organization of material and intellectual production. We want to give this principle the place that it deserves and reduce the role of competition.

2. Construct a world based on the full and complete affirmation of citizenship and equality between the sexes.

The citizen must have the ultimate responsibility for the management of all aspects of social, political, economic, and cultural life. That is the condition for an authentic democratization. Otherwise the human being is reduced to the status of a mere bearer of labor-power, a powerless spectator faced with decisions handed down by the authorities, and a consumer encouraged to be wasteful. The affirmation, in law and in fact, of the absolute equality of the sexes is an integral part of authentic democracy. One of the conditions of the latter is the eradication of all avowed or surreptitious forms of patriarchy.

3. Construct a universal civilization that offers the greatest possibility for the creative development of diversity in all area.

For neoliberalism, the affirmation of the individual—not the citizen—permits the best human qualities to flourish. The intolerable isolation that competition imposes on this individual in the capitalist system produces its illusory remedy: imprisonment in the ghetto of a supposed common identity, most often of the para-ethnic or para-religious type. We want to construct a universal civilization that looks toward the future without any nostalgia for the past. In this construction, the political diversity of citizenship and the diversity of cultural and political differences among nations and peoples become the means of providing individuals with strengthened capacities for creative development.

4. Construct socialization through democracy.

Neoliberal policies intend to impose a single mode of socialization through the market. However, the destructive effects of these policies for the majority of human beings no longer have to be demonstrated. The world that we want to build conceives of sociability as the principal result of unrestricted democratization. Within this framework, where the market can find its proper place, but not a predominant one, the economy and finance must be put at the service of a social plan and not unilaterally subjected to the demands of the uncontrolled development of capital's initiatives, which favor the particular interests of a tiny minority. The radical democracy that we want to promote reestablishes the creative force of political innovation as a fundamental human attribute. It bases social life on a diversity that is tirelessly produced and reproduced and not on a manipulated consensus that erases fundamental debates and confines dissidents into ghettos.

5. Construct a world based on the recognition of the non-commodity status of nature, the planet's resources, and agricultural lands.

The goal of the neoliberal capitalist model is to subject all aspects of social life, almost without exception, to commodity status. Privatization and excessive commodification lead to unprecedented devastating effects: destruction of biodiversity, ecological threats, waste of renewable and nonrenewable resources (petroleum and water in particular), annihilation of peasant societies threatened with massive expulsions from their lands. All these domains must be managed as the common wealth of humanity. In these spheres, decision-making should not, for the essential points, be a matter for the market but for the political powers of nations and peoples.

6. Construct a world based on recognition of the non-commodity status of cultural products, scientific knowledge, education, and health.

Neoliberal policies lead to the commodification of cultural products and the privatization of important social services, notably education and health. This choice entails the mass production of low-quality para-cultural products, the subjection of research to the exclusive priorities of short-term profitability, and the deterioration, perhaps even elimination, of education and healthcare for the popular classes. The renewal and expansion of public services must be guided by the objective of satisfying the need for and essential right to education, healthcare, and food.

7. Promote policies that closely combine unlimited democracy, social progress, and the affirmation of the autonomy of nations and peoples.

Neoliberal policies repudiate the specific requirements of social progress necessary for the correction of inequalities. Instead, social progress is supposedly produced spontaneously by the expansion of the markets. In these conditions, democracy is emptied of all effective content and made extremely vulnerable and fragile.

Affirming the objective of authentic democracy requires that social progress be given a decisive place in the management of all aspects of social, political, economic and cultural life. The diversity of nations and peoples produced by history, in its positive aspects as well as resulting inequalities, calls for the affirmation of their autonomy. There is no unique formula in the political and economic spheres that would allow us to overlook this autonomy. The objective of constructing equality necessarily requires a diversity of means to carry it out.

8. Affirm the solidarity of the peoples of the North and South in the construction of internationalism on an anti-imperialist foundation.

The solidarity of all peoples, North and South, in the construction of a universal civilization can not be based on the notion that, since everyone lives on the same planet, it should be possible to neglect the conflicts of interest between the different classes and nations that make up the real world. Such solidarity requires going beyond the laws and values of capitalism and the imperialism that is inherent to it. The regional organizations of the alternative globalization movement should support the view that the autonomy and solidarity of the nations and peoples on all five continents must be strengthened. This perspective contrasts with the viewpoint inherent in the current dominant models of regionalization, conceived of as so many constitutive blocs of neoliberal globalization. Fifty years after the Bandung Conference, the Bamako Appeal calls for a Bandung of the peoples of the South, those who are the victims of the expansion of really existing capitalism, and calls for a reconstruction of a peoples' front of the South that is capable of defeating the imperialism of the dominant economic powers and the military hegemony of the United States. This anti-imperialist front would not oppose the peoples of the South to those of the North. On the contrary, it is a foundation for the construction of a global internationalism that involves everyone in the building of a common civilization in its diversity.

III. LONG-TERM OBJECTIVES AND IMMEDIATE ACTION PROPOSALS

In order to move from collective awareness to the construction of collective, popular, diverse, and multipolar actors, it is necessary to identify precise themes for the formulation of concrete strategies and proposals. These themes, presented in more detail below, support one another without, however, totally overlapping, since the interconnections among them are many and varied. They cover the following ten areas, commensurate with long-term objectives and immediate action proposals: 1. The political organization of globalization; 2. The economic organization of the world system; 3. The future of peasant societies; 4. The construction of a united workers' front; 5. Regionalization for the peoples' benefit; 6. the democratic management of societies; 7. Equality between the sexes; 8. Management of the planet's resources; 9. Democratic management of the media and cultural diversity; and 10. Democratization of international organizations.

The Bamako Appeal is an invitation to all the organizations of struggle which represent the vast majorities that comprise the popular classes of the globe, to all those excluded from the neoliberal project, and to all people and political forces who support these principles to work together in order to put into effect a new collective conscience, as an alternative to the present system of inequality and destruction.

PROPOSALS OF THE BAMAKO APPEAL

Building synergies and solidarities beyond geographic and sectional boundaries is the only way to act in a globalized world and the only way to open up alternatives. Over the course of the year, working groups will continue to deepen and give concrete expression to the themes taken up below in order to summarize the situation again at the time of a new meeting and propose strategic priorities for action.

1. FOR A MULTIPOLAR WORLD SYSTEM BASED ON PEACE, LAW, AND NEGOTIATION

In order to imagine an authentic multipolar world system that rejects the control of the planet by the United States of America and guarantees all the rights of citizens and peoples to control their own destinies, it is necessary to:

I) Strengthen the movement opposing war and military occupations and strengthen solidarity with peoples engaged in resistance in the hotspots of the planet. In that regard, it is very important that the worldwide demonstrations against the war in Iraq and the military presence in Afghanistan anticipated for March 18 and 19, 2006 be linked with:

- Calls for prohibition on the use and manufacture of nuclear weapons and the destruction of all existing arsenals;
- Calls for dismantling of all military bases outside of national territory, in particular the base in Guantánamo;
- Calls for the immediate closure of all CIA prisons.

II) Reject NATO interventions outside of Europe and demand that the European partners dissociate themselves from U.S. preventive wars, while undertaking a campaign aimed at dissolving the organization.

III) Reaffirm solidarity with the people of Palestine, who symbolize resistance to world apartheid. The latter is clearly expressed by the wall that establishes the split between "civilization" and "barbarism." To this end, strengthening campaigns to demand demolition of this shameful wall and the withdrawal of Israeli troops from the occupied territories is a priority.

IV) Expand campaigns of solidarity with Venezuela and Bolivia as sites for the construction of alternatives to neoliberalism and architects of Latin American integration.

Beyond these campaigns, the following should be considered:

- The constitution of a network of researchers, working in close connection with militant groups acting at the local level, to form up-to-date and exhaustive databases about the military bases of the United States and NATO. Precise information on these military and strategic questions would make it possible to increase the effectiveness of campaigns undertaken for their dismantling;

• The creation of an observer group, an "Imperialism Watch," that would not only denounce wars and their propaganda but also all operations and pressures, economic and otherwise, carried out against peoples of the world;

• The creation of a worldwide anti-imperialist network that would coordinate mobilizations across the planet.

2. FOR A REORGANIZATION OF THE WORLD ECONOMIC SYSTEM

With the goal of developing an action strategy to transform the world economic system, it is necessary to:

1) Strengthen protest campaigns against the current operational rules of the World Trade Organization (WTO) and define alternative rules (in favor of removing agriculture, services, and intellectual property from consideration by the WTO);

2) Create work groups, in connection with social movements and organizations that have long been working on the items listed below, to establish dependably and exhaustively an inventory of proposals for alternative measures in the most fundamental economic areas:

• The organization of capital and technology transfers;

• Proposals for regulations (investment codes, for example) that specify the rights of nations and workers;

• The organization of the monetary system: control of the flow of capital (in particular speculative capital), suppression of tax havens, construction of regional systems for managing stock exchanges and their articulation in a reformed world system (calling into question the IMF and the World Bank, returning to the principle that nations have the primary right to define their economic system, abolition of the constraints imposed by the non-negotiable decisions of international organizations);

• The formulation of genuine legislation concerning external debts (requiring that states provide audits to permit identification of illegitimate debts) and, in the short term, strengthening of the mobilization calling for the cancellation of Third World debt;

• The reform of social services and their financing: education, health, research, retirement.

3) Create groups of specialized researchers to follow changes in capital movements and the mechanisms of the dependence of national financial capital on international financial capital;

4) Create working groups, with an Internet site and discussion groups, by country and region, to study the property structures and the operating mechanisms of capitalism in each country and in its relations with the international financial system;

5) Create places for journalist education to inform them about the complex mechanisms of neoliberal globalization;

6) Bring into contact, in the form of connected Internet sites, various organizations of progressive economists and militants involved in the search for alternatives to neoliberal globalization in each region of the world (Asia, Africa, Latin America, Oceania, Europe, North America).

3. FOR REGIONALIZATION THAT WORKS ON BEHALF OF THE PEOPLE AND STRENGTHENS THE SOUTH IN GLOBAL NEGOTIATIONS

Starting from the observation that free trade, by favoring the strongest, is the enemy of regional integration and that the latter cannot be achieved according to the rules of free trade, it is necessary to bring out the conditions for an alternative form of cooperation within each large region, like for example a revival of the Tricontinental, in close connection with the action of social movements.

• In Latin America, in the face of attacks by multinationals, workers have incorporated the question of regional integration into a new perspective, based on cooperative advantages and not on comparative advantages. Such is the case with alternative experiments in the South for cooperation concerning petroleum (Petrocaribe),[24] debt reduction (repurchase of debts among the countries of the South), and education and healthcare (Cuban doctors, for example). These are the political principles that must establish cooperation aimed at encouraging growth and solidarity in every country and not the rules imposed by the WTO.

• In Africa, the aspiration for unity is very strong, as is the awareness of the impossibility of isolated resistance or development, given the pressures of neoliberal globalization. Numerous institutions of integration are, however, ineffective and the most active are those inherited from the colonial and apartheid periods. The African Union and its economic and social program (NEPAD)[25] do not include any idea of collective resistance. It is in this context that civil societies must become aware of the necessity of overcoming their divisions.

For the North African countries of the Mediterranean region, the Euro-Mediterranean agreements are an additional example of regionalization carried out at the expense of the South.

• In Asia, in order to deal with neoliberal globalization, despite the difficulties, popular initiatives for another type of regional integration, bringing together a number of civil society organizations, NGOs, etc., have been undertaken in most countries, leading notably to the drawing up of a popular charter aimed at strengthening trade cooperation.

Consequently, it appears timely to recommend, beyond intensifying the campaigns against wars and threats of war, the following proposals:

1) For Latin America: expand the support campaigns for ALBA[26] in order to defeat the United States' ALCA[27] strategy decisively, promote independence and development in justice and equity among peoples, and construct an integration founded on cooperation and solidarity able to adapt to the specificities of the latter two desiderata; mobilize social movements for an expansion and intensification of alternative integration processes, of the Petrocaribe or TeleSUR[28] type; promote trade that is based on strategies of cooperation; and strengthen the links among social and political organizations in order to implement these recommendations.

2) For Africa: make the civil society movements aware of the necessity of formulating alternative proposals for African initiatives; take into account the necessity to coordinate the actions undertaken at the regional and national levels; launch campaigns

for peace to put an end to existing conflicts or avert the risks of new conflicts; abandon conceptions of integration based on race or culture.

3) For Asia: thwart the expansion and competition of capital between countries and reinforce solidarity between the popular classes of different countries; promote local circulation between production and consumption; promote the sciences for rural reconstruction.

To be effective, cooperation between countries of the South must express the solidarity of peoples and governments that, from the standpoint of a multipolar world system, are resisting neoliberalism and searching for alternatives.

4. FOR THE DEMOCRATIC MANAGEMENT OF THE PLANET'S NATURAL RESOURCES

The concept of "natural resources" must be subordinated to the concepts "sustainability" and "biodiversity," and thus ultimately to everyone's right to a decent life, in order to put an end to the devastation and plunder of the planet. What is involved then, is a vital principle and not simply management of natural resources. The latter cannot be used beyond their capacity for renewal, according to the needs of each country. Criteria for their use must be defined in order to guarantee sustainable development and preserve biodiversity and ecosystems. Thus the development of substitutes for non-renewable resources should be encouraged. The commodification of life results in wars for oil, water, etc. Agribusiness favors cultivation for profit over cultivation for subsistence needs, while imposing technical methods that result in dependence and destruction of the environment (farming contracts that require the use of certain equipment, fertilizers and seeds, such as GMO seeds).

In concrete terms, two levels of action on the environment must be combined: micro and macro. On the macro level, which concerns states, it would be desirable for an interstate framework for multilateral cooperation to have the ability to apply political pressure on states to take comprehensive measures. The micro level concerns local or regional actions, where civil society has an important role to play, particularly in distributing information and changing practices in order to save resources and protect the environment. The local level must be strengthened. Decisions are often made only with the macro level in mind.

The following actions could result from this:

1) The formation of an international tribunal responsible for considering ecological crimes: the countries of the North and their local clients could then be sentenced to pay reparations to the countries of the South (ecological debts);

2) The illegalization of any contracts that result in a dependence of farmers on those who provide seeds; such contracts lead to technological slavery and destruction of biodiversity;

3) The abolition of "pollution rights" and their market and the requirement of the wealthy countries to reduce their level of carbon dioxide emissions (5.6 tons per year per person in the United States) in order to allow the poor countries (0.7 tons per year per person for countries other than the G8 countries) to industrialize;

4) The prohibiting of the building of dams, insofar as they are really necessary, unless there is compensation for the displaced population (economic refugees);

5) The prevention of biological and genetic resources from being patented by the North, which impoverishes the countries of the South and is nothing but colonial-style pillaging;

6) The fighting of the privatization of water, such as promoted by the World Bank, even under the form of a private-public partnership (PPP), and the guarantee of a minimum quantity of water for each person while respecting the rate of renewal of groundwater;

7) The creation of an observation group, an "Ecological Watch," able to denounce and react against attacks on the environment.

5. FOR A BETTER FUTURE FOR PEASANT AGRICULTURE

In the area of peasant agriculture, there are, initially, medium and long-term objectives linked to food sovereignty, which are simultaneously at the national, international, multilateral (that of the WTO) and bilateral levels (Economic Partnership Agreements [EPAs], negotiated between the African, Caribbean and Pacific [ACP] countries and the European Union). At the national level, this also involves agricultural pricing and market policies as well as structural policy, such as the access of farmers to the means of production, starting with the land. In the short term, in 2006, it is necessary to prevent the completion of the Doha Round, which will make it easier to refuse to complete Economic Partnership Agreements. For that reason, the proposals here focus on two areas: the means to achieve food sovereignty in the medium-term and, as a preliminary step, the failure of the Doha Round and the Economic Partnership Agreements.

1) Proposals to achieve food sovereignty:

Food sovereignty is the right that should be granted to each state (or group of states) to define internal agricultural policy and the type of integration into the world economy it desires. This includes the right to protect itself effectively from imports and subsidize its farmers, on the condition that it is prohibited from exporting any agricultural products at a price that is lower than the average total production cost without direct or indirect subsidies (upstream or downstream). Food sovereignty is the lever that allows all countries to recover their national sovereignty in all areas. It is also a tool to promote democracy since it requires the participation of all forces in agro-food production in the definition of its objectives and means, beginning with family farmers. It thus implies regulatory action at the national, sub-regional, and international levels.

At the national level: States should guarantee peasant farmers access to productive resources, starting with the land. It is necessary to stop promoting agribusiness and the monopolization of land by the national bourgeoisie (including government officials) and transnational companies to the detriment of peasant farmers. This implies facilitating investments in family farms and making local products more attractive to consumers. Access to land for all peasants in the world must be recognized as a fundamental right. Its implementation requires appropriate reforms of landowning systems and sometimes it requires agrarian reforms.

In order to encourage urban consumers to share the objective of food sovereignty, an indispensable condition for government participation, three types of action should be undertaken:

• Restrict the activities of merchants that put farmers and consumers at a disadvantage.

• Carry out awareness campaigns for consumers on the immense harm done to agriculture and to the whole economy by dependence on imported agricultural products, which are practically the only ones sold, for example, in the supermarkets of West Africa.

• Gradually raise agricultural prices while increasing the right to import so as not to penalize consumers with very limited purchasing power. At the same time, that should be accompanied by the distribution of food coupons to consumers that allow them to purchase local foodstuffs at old prices, much like what is done in the United States, India, and Brazil, while waiting for an increase in the productivity of local farmers, which leads to lower unit production costs and allows them to lower their selling prices to consumers.

AT THE SUB-REGIONAL LEVEL: In order for states to be able to recover their full sovereignty, starting with food sovereignty, regional political integration is imperative for the small countries of the South. For that purpose, current regional institutions must be reformed, particularly, in Africa, UEMOA[29] and ECOWAS,[30] which are too dependent on various mega-powers.

AT THE INTERNATIONAL LEVEL: Put pressure on the United Nations to recognize food sovereignty as a fundamental right of states that is indispensable to implementing the right to adequate food defined by the 1948 Universal Declaration on Human Rights and the 1966 International Covenant on Economic, Social and Cultural

Rights. At this level, four instruments for regulating international agricultural trade should be established to make food sovereignty effective:

• An effective protection against irresponsible imports, based on variable levies that guarantee a fixed entry price in such a way as to assure minimum internal agricultural prices that would secure the investments of farmers and bank loans. Customs duties are insufficient protection against wildly fluctuating world prices, a fluctuation that is made worse by changing exchange rates.

• Elimination of all forms of dumping, by prohibiting all exports at prices that are below the average total cost of production of the country without direct or indirect subsidies.

• Mechanisms for international cooperation to control supply in such a way as to avoid structural overproduction and minimize conjunctural overproduction, which cause agricultural prices to collapse.

• The need to remove agriculture from the purview of the WTO by confiding international regulation of agricultural trade to a United Nations institution, possibly the FAO (Food and Agricultural Organization). In particular, by designing this organization on the tripartite model of the ILO (International Labor Organization), this institution would regulate trade by bringing together representatives of agricultural unions (IFPA and Via Campesina),[31] agro-food corporations (which already put pressure on governments negotiating at the WTO from behind the scene) and states.

2) Short-term proposals to prevent the completion of the Doha Round and Economic Partnership Agreements:

A major lesson of the WTO ministerial conference held in Hong Kong is that Brazil and India, and with them the G20, have distanced themselves from the interests of the populations of the Third World and revealed themselves to be the most determined promoters of neoliberal globalization. Since the Doha Round is a "single undertaking," there is a way to defeat it. International civil society, starting with the peasant organizations of the North and

South, could, in a media campaign, show that these subsidies (particularly those of the "green box")[32] are an instrument for much more sizeable dumping than explicit export subsidies and will be even more so beginning in 2014 when the latter are eliminated.

6. FOR THE CONSTRUCTION OF A UNITED FRONT OF WORKERS

Two main weapons in the hands of workers are the right to vote and the right to form unions. Democracy and unions, up to the present, have mainly been built on a national basis. However, neoliberal globalization is a challenge for workers over the entire world and global capitalism cannot be confronted only at the national level. Today, the task is twofold: strengthen the national level and simultaneously globalize democracy and reorganize a world working class.

Massive unemployment and the growing importance of informal labor are two other major reasons to rethink the existing organizations of the popular classes. A worldwide strategy for labor must consider not only the situation of workers who work under stable contracts. Employment outside formal sectors involves a growing part of the workforce, even in the industrialized countries. In most of the countries of the South, workers outside the formal sector, i.e., those with temporary jobs, those working in the informal sectors, the self-employed, the unemployed, street vendors, sellers of personal services, together form the majority of the popular classes. These groups are growing in most countries of the South because of high unemployment and because of an additional two-sided process: the scarcity and informality of guaranteed employment and the continuing exodus from rural areas. The most important task will be for workers outside the formal sector to organize and for traditional unions to be open to carrying out common actions with them.

Traditional unions find it difficult to deal with this challenge. Not every organization of workers outside the formal sectors will necessarily be a union or similar organization. The traditional unions will also have to change. New possibilities for working together, based on horizontal connections and mutual respect, must be developed between traditional unions and the new social movements. For that purpose, the following proposals are offered for consideration:

1) An opening of unions toward collaboration with other social movements without trying to subordinate the latter to the traditional union structure or to a specific political party.

2) The formation of effectively transnational union structures to deal with transnational employers. These union structures should have a capability to negotiate and a mandate to organize common actions beyond national borders. For that purpose, an important step would be to organize strong union structures within certain transnational corporations. The latter have a complex production network and are often very aware of any rupture in the production and distribution chains, which is an indication of their vulnerability. A few successes in struggles against transnational corporations could have a real impact on the world balance of power between capital and labor.

3) Technological development and structural change are necessary to improve living conditions and eradicate poverty, but relocations of production are not carried out today in the interest of workers, only according to profit motives. It is necessary to promote a gradual improvement of wages and working conditions, increase local production with local demand and devise a system for negotiating relocations as an alternative to the profit motive and free trade. These possible relocations could be part of negotiations with transnational corporations in order to avoid a situation where workers from different countries are forced to compete with one another in a relentless fight.

4) Consider the rights of migrant workers to be a fundamental concern of unions by ensuring that solidarity among workers is not linked to their national origin. Segregation and discrimination, whether on ethnic or other bases, are threats to the solidarity of the working class.

5) Ensure that the future transnational organization of the working class is not conceived as a single hierarchical and pyramidal structure, but rather that it is composed of a variety of differ-

ent types of organizations with a networked structure with numerous horizontal links.

6) Promote a reorganized labor front, with structures covering workers outside the formal sector throughout the world, which is capable of coordinated action to confront global capitalism effectively.

Such a comprehensive and revived worldwide movement of workers, acting together with other social movements could transform the present world and create a world order founded on solidarity rather than competition.

7. FOR A DEMOCRATIZATION OF SOCIETIES AS A NECESSITY FOR FULL HUMAN DEVELOPMENT

Progressive forces must re-appropriate the concept of democracy because an alternative, socialist society must be completely democratic. Democracy is not decreed from above. It is a process of cultural transformation because people transform themselves through their own activities. It is thus indispensable that activists in popular movements and in Left or progressive governments understand that it is necessary to create spaces for real participation in workplaces as well as in neighborhoods. Without the transformation of people into the real protagonists of their history, it will not be possible to resolve their problems: health, food, education, housing, etc. The fall of the socialist countries of Eastern Europe is closely associated with an absence of participation. The citizens of these countries were hardly motivated to defend regimes in which they were observers and not actors.

The struggle for democracy must also be linked to the struggle for the eradication of poverty and all forms of exclusion. If there is a serious desire to resolve these problems, then it is necessary that people actually wield power. That implies a struggle against capital's logic of profit and setting up, in spaces that can be taken over, a different logic, one that is humanist and based on solidarity. The mere assertion of the necessity for an alternative society is no longer sufficient and it is thus necessary to propose popular initiatives that are alternatives to capitalism and that strive to break with commodity logic and the relations that this dynamic requires.

But it is also a question of organizing struggles that are not reduced to mere economic demands, even if these are necessary, and that propose an alternative social project, including real levels of authority and democracy, which go beyond the current forms of representative, parliamentary, and electoral-based democracy. It is, thus, necessary to fight for a new type of democracy, coming from below for those on the bottom, based on local governments, rural communities, workers' fronts, citizens, etc. This democratic practice of solidarity will be the best way to attract new social sectors to a struggle for a fully democratic alternative society.

The following broad outline is offered of ways to give concrete expression to the principles set out here:

- Incorporate democracy into all aspects, individual and collective, of emancipation and liberation movements.
- Recognize that the failures of the Soviet system and the regimes arising from decolonization result, in part, from their denial of liberties and their underestimation of the importance of democracy. The elaboration of alternatives should include this observation and grant a primary place to constructing democracy.
- Contest the two-faced discourse of the dominant powers that are quick to give lessons in democracy. The cynicism of U.S. imperialism is particularly intolerable, as its agents reveal themselves to be warmongers, torturers, and violators of freedom. However, that should not serve as a pretext to limit freedoms and the practice of democracy.
- Challenge the dominant conception of democracy advanced by the United States and the Western powers. Democracy cannot be defined as accepting the rules of the market, subordination to the world market, multi-party elections controlled from abroad, and a simplistic ideology of human rights. This type of democracy consists of imposing the expansion of the market economy by linking it arbitrarily to the recognized importance of free elections and respect for rights. By restricting democracy in this way, its meaning is perverted.

• Recognize that there is a strong dialectic between political democracy and social democracy, because a political democracy is incomplete and cannot last if inequalities, exploitation, and social injustice continue. A social democracy cannot progress without struggling against oppression and discrimination, while keeping in mind that no social policy can justify the absence of freedoms and disrespect for fundamental rights.

• Affirm that democracy requires effective and growing participation of the population, of producers and inhabitants. This entails transparency in decision-making processes and responsibilities and does not negate the importance of representative democracy. On the contrary, it complements and deepens it.

• Since democracy should facilitate the fight against poverty, inequality, injustice, and discrimination, it must grant a strategic place to the poor and the oppressed, to their struggles and movements. In this sense, democracy in the operation of these movements contributes to their survival and successes.

• Democracy in the anti-globalization (or "alternative globalization") movement is an indication of the importance that the movement attaches to democracy in its work. This implies a reform of political and organizational culture, with particular attention granted to the question of authority and hierarchy. To that end, one of the immediate action proposals is to undertake a campaign to give an important place in popular education movements to citizen education and education for democracy to ensure that the democratic element be present in teaching.

We recall here that the alternative globalization movement is the vehicle for a fundamentally democratic project. It demands access to fundamental rights for everyone. These are, first, civil and political rights, particularly the rights to free organization and free expression, which are fundamental to democratic liberties.

Next, there are demands for the economic, social, cultural and environmental rights that are the foundation of social democracy. Lastly, there are demands for collective rights and the rights of peoples to fight against the oppression and violence imposed on them. The important question here is to define a program to implement democracy.

The alternative globalization movement also recognizes the importance of public services as one of the essential means to guarantee access to equal rights for everyone. It defends the struggles of workers and the users of public services. It puts forward proposals coming from movements for the defense of public services, particularly education and health services. For example, in health services, access to a list of free medicines and the rejection of monopolies, the dictatorship of patents and the attempt to patent living organisms.

• The struggle for democracy must take into account various levels for intervention. We will look at five of these levels: the company, local democracy, national democracy, large regions, and world democracy. By way of illustration, an action can be proposed for each of these levels. The choice of priorities will result from debate over strategies.

1) Democracy at the company level is a major demand. It implies recognition of the power of workers, consumers, and territorial and national public authorities. It requires the rejection of the dictatorship of stockholders and the destructive logic of finance capital. It results in control over decision-making, particularly concerning relocations. The innovative use of forms of self-organization and cooperation is one of the ways to assert the multiplicity of forms of production and reject the spurious proof offered for the effectiveness of private capitalist enterprise. The movement demanding social and environmental responsibility on the part of companies has much potential, despite the risks of co-optation, on the condition that it results in enforceable public regulations incorporated into international law.

2) Local democracy meets the demand for proximity and participation. It is based on local institutions that should guarantee public services and it promises an alternative to neoliberalism, preferring the local level and the satisfaction of needs to the adjustment of the entire society to the world market. It makes it possible to reform the notion of citizenship, particularly on the basis of residence and its consequences.

3) National democracy remains the strategic level. Questions of identity, borders, respect for the rights of minorities, and the legitimacy of institutions contribute to the foundations of popular sovereignty. Public policies can offer an arena for confronting neoliberalism. Redistribution of wealth based on taxation should be defended and expanded. Measures such as a minimum income and social security coverage based on solidarity across generations should not be restricted to the wealthy countries, but should be based on the division between profits and income from labor specific to each society.

4) Large regions can spread neoliberal globalization, as with the European Union, as well as counter-tendencies and places of resistance, such as demonstrated by Mercosur[33] and the failure of ALCA (FTAA). From this point of view, the Continental Social Forums have important responsibilities.

5) World democracy is a possible response to neoliberal globalization. Currently, the mobilizations with the highest priority to be carried by the anti-globalization movement are: cancellation of Third World debt; fundamentally calling into question the WTO; elimination of tax havens; international taxation, particularly on finance capital (capital transfers, profits of transnational corporations, eco-taxes, etc.); a radical reform of international financial institutions (based in particular on the principle of "one country, one vote"); reform of the United Nations based on respect for the rights of peoples and rejection of preventive war.

It would thus be necessary to organize a "Democracy Watch," which should be able to resist the hegemony of the dominant countries, above all the United States, and their fallacious discourse on democracy; encourage citizen control; and promote democratic forms invented and implemented by social and citizen movements.

8. FOR THE ERADICATION OF ALL FORMS OF OPPRESSION, EXPLOITATION, AND ALIENATION OF WOMEN

The forms of the patriarchy are multiple, like its bonds with imperialism and neoliberalism. It is important and necessary to analyze their effects on women. The concept of patriarchy refers to the domination of the father/patriarch and has been used to describe a family dominated by men who have authority over all other members of the family. This model is certainly not universal. A number of African societies have been matrilineal or based on dual lineages, patrilineal and matrilineal, with specific roles for individuals. This patriarchal system expanded with the growth of the Abrahamic religions and colonial ideologies and legislation. Today, patriarchy indicates above all male domination, inequality between the genders to the detriment of women and multiple forms of women's subordination. The family, which socializes the child, remains the primary site for the "domestication" of girls and women. This hierarchy of genders is all the more effective since it is supported by cultural norms and religious values that result in the appropriation of the productive and reproductive capabilities of women. The state reinforces this patriarchal power with its policies and its family codes.

Discrimination persists in relations within the family sphere, education, access to natural, material and financial resources, employment, participation in political power, etc. Despite a noticeable advance in the rights of women, male domination is still firmly in place in the institutions that reproduce neoliberal organizations.

Analysis of the relations between patriarchy and imperialism and the mixed results from the struggles of women against these systems lead to the following proposals for action:

1) Break with the marginalization of issues specific to women, which results in a political and scientific apartheid. Since the question of gender cuts across all areas of life, it must be taken into account in all recommendations.

2) Continue lobbying civil society and political organizations to strengthen the alliance between feminist organizations and

progressive forces and put on their agenda the defense of women, including:

• Fighting against the image of the inferior position of women in the social, political, cultural, and religious discourses of global society;

• Developing education and training of women in order to break the internalization of this position of inferiority;

• Disseminating a better awareness of the active role of women in society;

• Encouraging men to question male domination in order to deconstruct its mechanisms;

• Strengthening legal measures for effective equality between genders;

• Increasing the representation of women in institutions (parity).

3) Make the history of women visible, their individual and collective actions, notably:

• The project undertaken by various organizations to grant the 2005 Nobel Peace Prize to a thousand women (*mille femmes*) as representative of all women;

• The "Women Say No to War" campaign against the war in Iraq;

• Various campaigns on current topics or social projects.

4) Promote the fundamental right of women to control their bodies and minds and to control decisions about their life choices: education, employment, various other activities, including sexuality and pregnancy (right to contraception, pregnancy by choice, right to abortion). The bodies of women are the site of all kinds of oppression and violence.

5) Support theoretical investigations, on the basis of women's experiences, to confront male domination and strengthen women's perspectives on various questions affecting society, thereby opening new horizons for research and action. Women's perspectives need to be cultivated particularly on matters of population (as in the population Conference in Cairo in 1994) and on the environment (as in the Earth Summit in Rio de Janeiro in

1992), where women demand the right to live in a healthy environment.

6) Develop databases and an Internet site on the impact of imperialism and neoliberalism on women.

9. FOR THE DEMOCRATIC MANAGEMENT OF THE MEDIA AND CULTURAL DIVERSITY

1. For the right to education:

Prior to the right to culture, the right to information and the right to inform, the fundamental problem of the right to education should be posed. This right, while it is officially recognized everywhere, remains ineffective in numerous countries, particularly for girls. It is thus a priority for all social movements to pressure governments to fulfill their basic obligations in this area.

2. For the right to information and the right to inform:

• Initiatives toward large media.

The right to information and the right to inform are in contradiction with the general logic of the media system. As a result of its growing concentration on the world level, it is not only a direct participant in and beneficiary of the mechanisms of neoliberal globalization but also a purveyor of its ideology. We have to fight tooth and nail to interfere with this "formatting" of human minds, which wants to make the neoliberal order acceptable, something inevitable and even desirable. To this end, campaigns should be launched in each country, within the framework of international cooperation:

• For legislative initiatives that aim at fighting against the concentration of the media;

• For legislative initiatives that aim at guaranteeing the autonomy of editorial staff in relation to shareholders and owners by encouraging, where they do not already exist, the creation of associations of journalists with real power to act;

• For education about media criticism in the school system and in popular organizations;

• Encourage alternative media.

Nonprofit alternative media, in every form (paper, radio,

television, Internet), already play an important role in providing multiple sources of information that are not subject to the dictates of finance and the multinationals. This is why it should be demanded of governments that they provide regulatory and tax conditions that benefit these media. A watchdog group, an "Alternative Media Watch," could identify the most progressive legislation currently existing in the world. Following the example of what the owners and managers of the large media do, it would be useful to organize a meeting of those who manage the alternative media from across the world each year, possibly within the framework of the World Social Forums.

• Do not allow the television networks of the North to monopolize images of the world.

The large international television networks of the North, such as CNN, have long benefited from a *de facto* monopoly and have provided a view of the world that corresponds to the interests of the dominant powers. In the Arab world, the creation of *al-Jazeera* has made it possible, with great professionalism, to break with the unilateral view of conflicts in the Middle East. The recent launching of TeleSUR allows Latin America to no longer to see itself only through the prism of U.S. media. The creation of an African network would meet the same need, and all efforts should be made to see that it happens.

3. For the right to express oneself in one's own language:

The first way to recognize all the "off-shore" elites of the planet is by their use of English. There is a logical connection between voluntary or resigned submission to the U.S. superpower and the adoption of its language as the sole tool of international communications. Currently, Chinese and the Romance languages, if mutual comprehension among them were promoted and, tomorrow, Arabic have as much right to play this same role. This is a matter of political will. In order to fight against an "all-English" world, the following measures should be encouraged:

• Education systems should have the objective, when conditions permit, of teaching two foreign languages (and not only English) for active and passive competence (comprehension, speaking, reading, writing) and one or two other languages for passive competence (reading and oral comprehension).

• Education systems should put into practice methods for mutual comprehension of Romance languages (Spanish, Catalan, French, Italian, Portuguese, Romanian, which are official languages in sixty countries). Communication is most effective when each person speaks his or her own language and understands that of his or her conversational partner;

• In the specific case of Africa, make the teaching and promotion of national languages a political priority of the African Union;

• Create an international fund to support the translation of the maximum number of documents into the languages of countries with few resources, in particular for accessibility on the Internet.

10. FOR THE DEMOCRATIZATION OF INTERNATIONAL ORGANIZATIONS AND THE INSTITUTIONALISATION OF A MULTIPOLAR INTERNATIONAL ORDER

The United Nations is an institution of peoples. In this respect, it is a positive advance for humanity. But it is also reflects the balance of power among states, the impact of which can turn out to be ambivalent, perhaps even negative in the case of certain peoples or in certain circumstances. Changes in the UN are thus necessary, insofar as the hegemony of the most powerful countries enables them to use the UN for their own purposes. Consequently, the following initiatives are proposed:

1. Democratize the United Nations;

2. Initiate reforms of the United Nations with the goal of limiting the inequalities resulting from the balance of power among states;

3. Bring pressure to bear on the governments that make up the UN. To accomplish this, form an observation group in each country that holds its government accountable for its actions within the United Nations, specialized agencies, and the organizations created at Bretton Woods (IMF, World Bank, WTO);

4. Refinance specialized organizations such as the FAO or WHO so as to avoid their dependence on transnational corporations;

5. Ensure the extended and effective presence of social movements and non-governmental organizations within international institutions;

6. Promote the International Courts of Justice, in particular concerning economic crimes, while preventing their exploitation by the dominant powers. At the same time, form courts of popular opinion in order to promote alternative ways to establish justice;

7. To democratize the United Nations, increase the power of the General Assembly and democratize the Security Council in order to break the monopoly of the nuclear powers (right to veto);

8. Promote a United Nations that allows for the formation of regional organizations with real powers on the different continents. In particular, promote a Middle East Social Forum, gathering together the progressive forces of the countries in the region to search for alternative solutions to the U.S. project of a Greater Middle East;

9. Promote within the United Nations respect for the sovereignty of nations, especially against the actions undertaken by the IMF, World Bank, and WTO;

10. Promote a World Assembly of Peoples to bring humanity out of the vicious cycle of poverty.

NOTES

1. The 1955 Bandung Conference was the first large-scale Afro-Asian conference held to oppose both sides in the Cold War, oppose any form of colonialism or neo-colonialism, and promote economic development of the African and Asian countries.—Trans.

2. The Tricontinental Conference was a meeting of Leftists in Havana in 1966 with the aim of supporting Third World liberation struggles. The Organization for Solidarity with the People of Asia, Africa and Latin America was established subsequent to this meeting and still exists, with headquarters in Havana.—Trans.

3. Samir Amin, *Obsolescent Capitalism: Contemporary Politics and Global Disorder* (London: Zed Press, 2004).

4. A radical journal published in Paris under the editorship of Maxime Rodinson, French Marxist and Middle East scholar.—Trans.

5. The theory of revolution and guerilla warfare inspired by Ernesto "Che" Guevara.—Trans.

6. The term refers to radical revolutionary groups that developed out of the communist movements of India, generally following a Maoist ideological line.—Trans.

7. The Qawmiyin movement was a group of young revolutionaries that attempted to combine Marxism, Maoism, and Guevarism. They initiated the formation of radical parties in Palestine (Naief Hawatmeh's Democratic Front and George Habash's Popular Front) and inspired the popular revolution in South Yemen.—Trans.

8 Khalid Bakdash (1912–1995) was the head of the Syrian Communist Party from 1936 until his death.—Trans.

9. I refer the reader to Samir Amin, *Beyond US Hegemony? Assessing the Prospects for a Multipolar World* (London: Zed Press, 2006), chapter 2, and "Théorie et pratique du projet chinois de socialisme de marché," *Alternatives Sud* (8:1, 2001).

10. Samir Amin, *The Future of Maoism* (New York: Monthly Review Press, 1983).

11. Ibid.

12. See Samir Amin, *Obsolescent Capitalism*.

13. See Samir Amin, ed., *Les luttes paysannes et ouvrières face aux défies du XXIe siècle* [Peasants' and Workers' Struggles Faced with the Challenges of the 21st Century] (Paris: Les Indes Savantes, 2005).

14. That is, different groups alternate holding power, though they all subscribe to the same basic political worldview. This should be viewed in contrast to a situation where true alternatives are posed.—Trans.

15. As will become clear below, the "our" here does not, for the most part at least, refer to the United States.—Trans.

16. "*Les clercs trahissent*" is an allusion to Julien Benda's 1927 book *La Trahison des clercs* (*The Treason of the Intellectuals*) (New Brunswick, NJ: Transaction Publishers, 2007).—Trans.

17. *Gemeinschaft* is often translated as "community" and *gesellschaft* as "society" or "civil society."—Trans.

18. In *The Liberal Virus* (New York: Monthly Review Press, 2004).

19. *Contrat première embauche*, translated as "first employment contract." This was a new form of employment contract pushed by the Villepin government in 2006. It would have made it easier for employers to fire employees under age twenty-six. The act was rescinded after massive protests.—Trans.

20. Two left-leaning, socialist-type organizations that were part of the broad coalition that brought about the fall of the Shah's regime. —Trans.

21. *Banlieue* is the French term for "suburb." However, in France the situation of the suburbs is quite different than in the United States. Many suburbs of

large French cities are inhabited by low-income, underemployed or unemployed people of immigrant origin. Conditions are similar to those conjured up by the term "inner city" in English.—Trans.

22. Mawdudi (1903–1979) was a Pakistani journalist, theologian, and political philosopher. He founded the Jamaat-e-Islami Islamic political party.—Trans.

23. A different verion of the Bamako Appeal may be found at the Third World Forum website (http://forumtiersmonde.net/fren/index.htm).—Trans.

24. An oil alliance between the Caribbean and Venezuela for the purchase of oil on preferential terms.—Trans.

25. New Partnership for Africa's Development.—Trans.

26. Bolivarian Alternative for the Americas (Alternativa Bolivariana para los Pueblos de Nuestra América).–Trans.

27. Area de Libre Comercio de las Américas (Free Trade Area of the Americas—FTAA).—Trans.

28. La Nueva Televisora del Sur (New Television Station of the South), a Latin American television network based in Caracas.—Trans.

29. Union économique et monétaire ouest-africaine (West African Economic and Monetary Union).—Trans.

30. Economic Community of Western African States.—Trans.

31. IFAP stands for the International Federation of Agricultural Producers. Via Campesina is an international movement of peasants, landless, and agricultural workers. —Trans.

32. See this website for the official definitions of the various subsidy "boxes" www.wto.org/english/tratop_e/agric_e/agboxes_e.htm. —Trans.

33. Mercado Común del Sur (Southern Common Market).—Trans.

INDEX